Puzzle Paragraphs

Taking the Mystery Out of Writing Nonfiction

Written by Christine Boardman Moen

Illustrated by Corbin Hillam

Teaching & Learning Company

1204 Buchanan St., P.O. Box ▮
Carthage, IL 62321-0010

This book belongs to

_____

Copyright © 2007, Christine Boardman Moen

ISBN 13: 978-1-57310-522-4

ISBN 10: 1-57310-522-8

Printing No. 987654321

Teaching & Learning Company
1204 Buchanan St., P.O. Box 10
Carthage, IL 62321-0010

The purchase of this book entitles teachers to make copies for use in their individual classrooms only. This book, or any part of it, may not be reproduced in any form for any other purposes without prior written permission from the Teaching & Learning Company. It is strictly prohibited to reproduce any part of this book for an entire school or school district, or for commercial resale. The above permission is exclusive of the cover art, which may not be reproduced.

All rights reserved. Printed in the United States of America.

TLC10522 Copyright © Christine Boardman Moen

Table of Contents

Dear Teacher or Parent,

Puzzle Paragraphs evolved from an action research project my eighth-grade students and I conducted. The project was called "Reading and Writing in the Real World," and the results were published in the Winter 2005-2006 edition of the *Illinois Reading Council Journal*.

My students learned from this project that knowing how to read and write well are essential, life-long skills. Additionally, at the conclusion of the project, students realized that reading and writing on a daily basis would continue beyond their high school and college careers because all professions and occupations require at least some degree of reading and writing. Indeed, my students were amazed to discover that such diverse professions and occupations as dentists, firefighters and even Hollywood stunt people had to read and write each and every day.

While my students' awareness increased substantially, I also learned the kinds of adjustments I needed to make in my instruction in order to prepare them for the reading and writing tasks of their futures. Most importantly, I realized that my students needed to read more informational texts and learn to recognize different types of text structures. Moreover, my students needed to utilize those same text structures in their own writing.

Consequently, I decided to utilize the paragraph format to introduce my students to informational text reading and writing. I chose the paragraph format because of two constraints that many middle school teachers face. First, many of us already have overloaded "must-teach-and-must-test" curricula, and the paragraph format allows for an easier inclusion than extensive inquiry projects. Moreover, many middle school teachers often teach up to 120 different students each day. By using the paragraph format, students can learn to read and write several different types of informational texts and the teacher can manage the reading and writing demands of the paragraph format while also assisting students with other pieces such as research papers, poetry, narratives and persuasive editorials.

Each of the 10 different puzzle paragraphs in this book serves as a mental template, or a structural starting point, for students to learn how to read and write informational text. These starting points are especially important for striving readers and writers as well as English Language Learners (ELL students) who need explicit models.

Please feel free to utilize the materials in this book to meet the needs of your student population and the needs of your curricula. Adapt, change, delete, add—do whatever you need to do to make the material work for you.

Sincerely,

Christine

Christine Boardman Moen
www.chrismoen.com

TLC10522 Copyright © Christine Boardman Moen

Puzzle Paragraphs: The Missing Pieces in Reading-Writing Classrooms

Readers' and writers' workshops have been a part of many classroom landscapes for nearly 20 years. In fact, the biggest impact of readers' and writers' workshops has been to transform classrooms into a place where students and teachers use reading to inform writing and writing to inform reading. Because each classroom is a unique learning community, many adaptations and variations have occurred to the approaches of readers' and writers' workshops. However, the basic and broadest elements of the workshop remain the same.

In Readers' Workshop

- Teachers teach students reading strategies.
- Students read independently and/or in guided reading groups.
- Students respond to their reading either orally or in writing.

In Writers' Workshop

- Teachers teach students writing strategies.
- Students spend time writing and conferencing with the teacher and others.
- Students publish and/or share their writing with others.

Utilizing readers' and writers' workshops in my classroom allows me to differentiate instruction, provides students choice in what they read and write, and encourages students to be self-directed learners. Most importantly, with readers' and writers' workshops, I utilize a variety of instructional practices.

- In readers' workshop, students do everything from practicing fluency by performing readers' theater scripts to learning how to choose a good book for independent reading.

- In writers' workshop, students also engage in a variety of activities. Some activities are small in scope, such as learning how to begin a sentence with a prepositional phrase. Other activities, such as writing a five-page research paper, are much more involved and take a great deal longer.

- One component that I have recently included in readers' and writers' workshops is what I call Puzzle Paragraphs. Puzzle Paragraphs offer students opportunities to read and write various structured informational texts in short, manageable lengths in order to understand and to imitate the functions and forms of these same types of informational texts.

The reading and writing classroom conference.

Informational Reading and Writing in the Real World

Informational texts, long pushed aside in many classrooms by narrative fictional texts, are steadily finding their rightful place in the instructional landscape of most classrooms. One reason for this shift is that the quality of informational texts has greatly improved over the last several years and is being acknowledged by professional educators' organizations. The National Council of Teachers of English presents the *Orbis Pictus Award* for Outstanding Nonfiction for Children. The American Library Association gives the ALSC/Robert F. Sibert Informational Book Award. (See Appendix A for a full list of organizations that give awards for quality informational texts.)

Another reason reading informational text is on the increase is that research indicates that standardized tests administered to students across the United States are comprised of anywhere from 50 to 85 percent informational texts. Additionally, research indicates that adults read mostly nonfiction (Calkins, Montgomery, Santman, and Falk 1998). It was this last portion of the research—that adults read mostly nonfiction as well as an action research project my students and I completed—that led me to include Puzzle Paragraphs in my Readers' and Writers' Workshops.

I entitled the action research project "Reading and Writing in the Real World: An IRC Grant-Funded Project Opens Students' Eyes," and it was published as a journal article.

1. First, I received a grant from the Illinois Reading Council, a state-wide literacy organization which is also affiliated with the International Reading Association.

2. As part of the project, my students wrote to people in different professions and occupations and asked them to describe the reading and writing activities they performed in their jobs.

3. After receiving the letters, students charted the myriad reading and writing activities and drew some conclusions about the types of required reading and writing activities of various professions and occupations.

As the title of the article states, it "open[ed] students' eyes." My students learned that everyone from the person who paints cars to the farmer who plows the fields to the stunt coordinator who performs in Hollywood movies reads and writes a lot every single day.

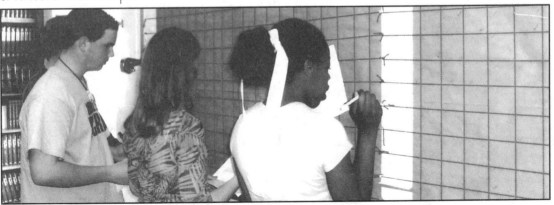
Students chart their data.

TLC10522 Copyright © Christine Boardman Moen

Not only did my students and I learn about the amount of reading and writing people do in their professions and occupations, but we also learned about the variety of reading and writing that different professions and occupations require.

- Students learned that many people in the working world read a lot of magazines, journals, work-related books, handbooks, manuals and instructions.

- They learned that people in the workplace don't do a lot of cover-to-cover reading but instead often read short, specific, need-to-know types and portions of texts.

- Students also discovered that a lot of writing done is often short and usually a means to inform the reader.

- Students learned that people in the working world write a lot of letters and e-mails, reports, logbooks, journal entries, forms, applications, instructions and handouts.

As a result of the action research project, I concluded that:

- I needed to provide students with activities that involved reading informational texts that in turn informed their writing of informational texts.

- These activities also had to be short enough to allow students to pursue a wide variety of reading and writing activities of other genres and formats in readers' and writers' workshops.

- These snapshot activities also had to fit with what I was already doing in my classroom; they couldn't be another add-on to an already busy schedule.

- Equally important, the reading and writing activities had to be manageable in length for middle school teachers who often see over 100 twelve-, thirteen- and fourteen-year-old students each day.

Types of Puzzle Paragraphs

I chose the 10 different Puzzle Paragraphs for this book by analyzing the most common types of expository text structures, reviewing various paragraph types, and by making appropriate selections from the ways in which paragraph details are arranged. Consequently, this book is a hybrid that blends text structure, paragraph types and arranging paragraph details. By doing this, I was able to select from the best that research had to offer and to blend that information to create workable reading and writing instruction to enable students to become better readers and writers of basic, expository-structured informational texts.

- First, I looked at various reports describing expository **text structures**. Meyers (1975) identified the following text structure patterns: cause-effect, comparison-contrast, problem-solution, description and collection. Young (2002) categorized text into descriptive, temporal sequence, definition/example, time sequence, list, cause and effect, comparison and contrast and problem and solution. Wormeli (2005) identified the following text structures: enumeration, chronological order, compare-contrast, cause and effect, and problem and solution.

- Next, I combed through various writing manuals, textbooks and guides popular with many middle school teachers. I found Kemper, Sebranek, and Meyer (2001)—a series with which I was familiar—to have an almost satisfying list and description of **paragraph types** and **arrangement of paragraph details**. The types of paragraphs this series describes include expository, descriptive, narrative and persuasive while the list of ways in which details can be arranged in

paragraphs includes classification, order of location, chronological order, explaining a process, illustration, climax, cause and effect and comparison. One arrangement of paragraph details that was missing from the Kemper, Sebranek, and Meyer's list was arranging details in order of importance, so I added that arrangement type myself.

- As you can see from Figure 1 (page 9), all three of the categories—text type, paragraph type and the arrangement of details in paragraphs—overlap in several areas. For example, cause and effect is described both as a text structure and a way to arrange details in a paragraph. At the same time, *descriptive* is a term that is used both as a text structure and a paragraph type.

What Puzzle Paragraphs offers in the midst of all this information is a structural starting point—a foothold for students to practice reading and writing several types of basic, expository-structured informational texts.

With Puzzle Paragraphs, students pour their ideas into "containers" called cause-effect paragraphs, problem-solution paragraphs and so forth—just like poets pour their ideas into structures called sestinas, pantoums and sonnets.

At the same time, using Puzzle Paragraphs is similar to using picture books and other types of texts as models for student reading and writing—only with Puzzle Paragraphs, the reading and writing activities provide success for students who need consistent, easy-to-understand and easy-to-follow examples of basic, expository-structured informational texts.

TLC10522 Copyright © Christine Boardman Moen

Figure 1

Text Structure	Paragraph Details	Paragraph Types
• cause-effect	• classification	• expository
• comparison-contrast	• location	• narrative
• problem-solution	• chronological order	• persuasive
• description	• explaining a process	• descriptive
• collection	• illustration	
• descriptive	• climax	
• temporal sequence	• cause and effect	
• definition/example	• comparison	
• time sequence	• order of importance	
• list		

In *How Writing Works: Imposing Organizational Structure Within the Writing Process*, author Gloria Houston (Pearson, 2004, page 10) discusses text structure and its connection to reading and writing: "If writing and reading are indeed two sides of the same coin, the writer must place the pattern there first if the reader is to make use of the same patterns to discern meaning."

With Puzzle Paragraphs, students look for structure when they read and manipulate the example paragraphs. In turn, when students write, they organize their ideas using the same structures they encountered in their reading.

I am convinced that this type of reading and writing will serve students well when they read and write not only in school but also in the workplace.

My synthesis of these categories led me to include the following informational text paragraphs in this book:

Paragraph Developed with Examples
Pages 36-40
Students select a topic that can be developed with three specific examples supported with three specific details.

Paragraph Developed with Facts
Pages 41-45
Students select five relevant and significant facts about a topic and weave these facts into a paragraph.

Paragraph Developed with Reasons
Pages 46-50
Students select a topic that can be developed with three specific reasons supported with three specific details.

Paragraph Developed with Cause-Effect
Pages 51-55
Students describe the relationship between an event or phenomena and its results. To do this, students describe the event or phenomena in the first portion of the paragraph and describe the results or connection in the last portion of the paragraph.

Paragraph Developed with Problem-Solution
Pages 56-60
Students describe a problem in the first part of the paragraph and describe a workable solution in the second part of the paragraph.

Paragraph Developed with Comparison-Contrast
Pages 61-71
Students use a statement of similarity, which states the three general similarities between the two subjects being compared and contrasted. Then students proceed to provide detailed contrasts of these three similarities. In an alternative format, students describe the similarities between the two subjects in the first half of the paragraph and the differences between the two subjects in the second half of the paragraph. The first paragraph uses a one-to-one contrast format, and the latter paragraph uses a block format.

Paragraph Developed with a List
Pages 72-76
Students select five to seven interesting details about a topic and weave those details into a paragraph.

Paragraph Developed with Definitions
Pages 77-81
Students choose a word and define it by using four to six example definitions.

Paragraph Developed with Sequence
Pages 82-86
Students describe an event by selecting pertinent details and arranging them in chronological order.

Paragraph Developed with How-To Steps
Pages 87-91
Students describe how to do something in step-by-step fashion.

TLC10522 Copyright © Christine Boardman Moen

Providing structure can be a positive, powerful instructional instrument. As Flood, Lapp, and Farnan point out, "As students attempt to control structure through writing, they gain insight into the fact that writers organize their information to maximize the reader's comprehension." (1986, page 558). As I explain to my students: Writers write to help readers read.

The fact that writers write for specific readers was very evident in the responses my students received during our action research project. People in various professions and occupations often noted that when they wrote something, they wrote for someone other than themselves. In fact, they noted that they wrote to be understood by a reader who was not able to sit next to him or her and ask clarifying question.

Students learned that people in the workplace wrote:

- to provide customers and clients with examples of their products or services.
- to compare and contrast their products and services with another company's.
- to offer workable solutions to problems.
- to chronicle the sequence of events that took place or will take place.
- to explain cause and effect (such as the cause of a fire and its resulting damage).
- to describe a list of products and services.
- to define a company's or organization's mission.

Extracting Information from Texts:
Lift It, Sift It, Sort It, Organize It

In addition to writing with a specific audience in mind, students also discovered that in the world of work, people read for a specific purpose. Of course, setting a purpose for reading is a readers' workshop mini-lesson. But this mini-lesson took on new meaning when it came to informational texts.

- First, students discovered that a worker set a purpose for reading that depended upon the task he or she was trying to accomplish, and the selection of reading material was dependent upon the purpose for reading.

- As a result, students discovered that in real-world reading, people often do not do the cover-to-cover type of reading that is expected in school.

- In addition, what people read as part of their work responsibilities often made its way into what they wrote. In other words, reading was often the basis for writing.

At the same time, workplace activities also found their way into people's writing.

- For example, firefighters, police officers and the coroner wrote reports of fires, accidents and deaths.

- Chemists, dance instructors and horse trainers often wrote in logbooks and journals.

- A worker might have to take notes during a meeting or presentation and then write a brief summary or proposal from his or her notes.

Consequently, I needed to find a balance to help my students quickly recognize a specific type of text structure in their reading but also be able to utilize that same text structure in their own writing. I had to establish a reading-to-write, writing-to-read connection. I decided to teach students text structure by providing them with paragraphs based on the different types of writing that people performed most often in the workplace and which are most often required in school—especially in content-area writing assignments.

Additionally, I knew I would have to teach students how to take information from their reading as well as from what I call "on-site activities" and put this information into their writing in a meaningful way. For example, people in the real world need to gather information and data and weave this into such things as letters and reports. At the same time, people in the real world make observations about events and work-related activities and weave this information into such things as letters, reports, logbooks and journals.

TLC10522 Copyright © Christine Boardman Moen

Here are three different ways in which I use information-gathering activities for students' written paragraphs. (Some of these student paragraphs appear in the Appendix.)

1. When students worked on the How-To Puzzle Paragraph, they assembled a small 20-piece puzzle. While doing this, they recorded the steps they followed and then wrote a paragraph describing how to put together a puzzle. I consider assembling a puzzle and writing a how-to paragraph an example of an on-site activity, which is an activity that a person in the workplace engages in to gather information through observation, experimentation and hands-on.

2. Another type of information-gathering activity involves students using more than one source. Taking information from different sources and synthesizing them to create a written document of some sort happens all the time in the work world. To do this synthesizing, students read *The Outsiders* by S.E. Hinton and then watched the Francis Ford Coppola movie of the same name. Students identified similarities and differences between the book and the movie and wrote a comparison-contrast paragraph.

3. A final type of information-gathering activity students engage in also relates to real-world reading and writing. Often people read information and then use this information to write proposals, reports, instructions and other types of documents. To teach students to extract information from their reading in order to use this information in some type of writing, I teach students a process called **Lift It, Sift It, Sort It, Organize It**.

Busy people in the workplace skim and scan information when they read. They underline or highlight important points and slow down their reading when the text is more difficult or if it contains especially relevant information. These skills are important mini-lessons for readers' workshop, but these skills and this process of reading also have implications for writers' workshop—to get information to use in their writing, readers must lift, sift, sort and organize information from text.

Lift It, Sift It, Sort It, Organize It is a process I have used for many years in my own writing, but one whose nifty, student-friendly title is based on information presented by McKenzie (2000), Harvey (1998) and Portalupi and Fletcher (2001).

- To teach students to Lift It, Sift It, Sort It, Organize It, I model the process several times by using newspaper articles, magazine articles or a brief section from a nonfiction book.

- Each student gets a copy of the text and a copy of the form which appears in Figure 2 (page 14). (The student copy, which you can duplicate, appears in the Appendix.)

- Finally, I make an overhead transparency of the form also so students and I can work together as a group to complete the process.

TLC10522 Copyright © Christine Boardman Moen

Figure 2

Lift It, Sift It, Sort It, Organize It

Read It   Carefully read the text. Read it a second time. Think!

Lift It   Select important details from the text and briefly record them on the
                   lines provided.

Sift It   Read the details you've selected and put a star or check mark by the
                   ones you think are the most important to include in your paragraph.

Sort It   Ask yourself:
                   • What does all this information add up to?
                   • What does this information say about the topic?
                   • What will I be trying to tell the reader with this information?

                   Next, review your graphic organizer and then ask:
                   • How does this information fit onto the organizer?

Organize It   After you record your information onto the organizer, ask yourself:
                   • Have I recorded the information in the correct areas on the organizer?
                   • Do I have enough information?
                   • Do I need to return to the text and/or my notes and select even
                     more information?

Title/author/source of your information: _____

_____

Sift It   **Lift It**

_____   _____

_____   _____

_____   _____

_____   _____

_____   _____

_____   _____

_____   _____

_____   _____

_____   _____

TLC10522 Copyright © Christine Boardman Moen

To Teach Lift It, Sift It, Sort It, Organize It

1. First, as students follow along, I **read aloud** the information, making connections and clarifying statements just like you would if you were teaching students think-alouds.

2. In the **Lift It** step, I lift details from the article and record them on the lines.

3. In the **Sift It** step, I sift through the details and put stars or check marks next to the most significant details, which should be the ones I want to include in my paragraph.

4. In the next step, **Sort It**, I sort the information by once again modeling a think-aloud and asking myself, "What do I have now?," "What kind of paragraph would this information fit into?" and "What am I trying to tell the reader with this information?"

5. In the **Organize It** step, I organize the information onto a paragraph graphic organizer to test whether I have enough information for a paragraph and if I am using the appropriate paragraph type for the information I have.

6. In addition to helping students extract information, I also want students to note the source or sources from which they extract their information.

- It is essential that students identify the source of their information in order to avoid plagiarism and to have a record of where they got their information in case they ever need to go back and double-check their information for the sake of clarity or completion.

- Most importantly, it is never too early to model integrity when citing sources.

A Source Information Record form that you can duplicate appears in the Appendix.

Attention-Getters in Informational Text Paragraphs

One component of the informational text paragraph that may not appear in other paragraph writing instruction is what I call the attention-getter. This attention-getter is similar to the grabber that students are taught to write as part of their introductory paragraph for longer papers.

In essays and research papers, students are taught to write a grabber and place it in their introductory paragraph prior to their thesis statement. With Puzzle Paragraphs, students write attention-getters and place them in front of their paragraph's topic sentence. As a result, each informational text paragraph has a mini introduction that serves as an example to follow when students proceed to writing longer papers. Thus the attention-getter allows students to write well-written stand-alone paragraphs.

*Attention-getters are optional. If you don't want to use these devices in your Puzzle Paragraphs—especially if reading and writing them are confusing to ELL or special needs students—skip them! Each paragraph will stand alone without an attention-getter. Students will simply begin each paragraph with a topic sentence.

TLC10522 Copyright © Christine Boardman Moen

Different Types of Attention-Getters

Students learn six different attention-getters they can use to open their paragraphs. Of course, students are not limited to these six. In fact, students often create their own unique ways of beginning their writing.

To acquaint students with attention-getters:

1. I give each student a list of the six examples and assign him or her a section of the library.

2. He or she reads the first paragraph of books in the assigned section and tries to find an example of each of the six.

3. Once the student finds an appropriate example, he or she records the author's words under the appropriate example heading.

This photograph shows students hard at work looking for attention-getters.

By having students read the opening sentences and paragraphs in a variety of fiction and nonfiction books, they not only come to recognize the six basic types of attention-getters they are encouraged to use in their own writing, but they also recognize that authors use a variety of different openers to get a reader's attention from the very first sentence in the book.

In the sample attention-getters that follow, the first comes from paragraphs that appear in this book. These are paragraphs that I wrote and use with students in readers' workshop. The second comes from students. One of their writers' workshop activities was to investigate various science fair project books and write a paragraph developed with examples describing three possible topics for their project.

Types and Examples of Attention-Getters

Ask a Question

1. What mammal, besides human beings, baby-sits an other's children, risks its life to save a friend, and cares for sick relatives? The answer is the world's biggest land animal: the elephant.

      (Paragraph Developed with Comparison-Contrast, page 61)

2. Does science fair equal science scare? Eighth-grade science fair doesn't have to be scary if you choose a suitable topic.

      Shelly

Single Word or a Series of Phrases

1. Tall, taller, tallest. When it comes to the world's towers, some are tall, others are taller and a very few are the tallest of all.

      (Paragraph Developed with Examples, page 36)

2. Animals. Plants. Minerals. Choosing a science fair topic takes some thinking.

      Jordon

Dialogue or Quotation

1. ". . . a wave of the rider's hand . . . and man and horse burst past . . . and go swinging away like a belated fragment of a storm." Author Mark Twain used these words in 1861 to describe a Pony Express rider that rode past the stagecoach Twain was traveling on through Nevada.

      (Paragraph Developed with Facts, page 41)

2. "These boots are made for walking" are words from a song that was famous many years ago. However, tennis shoes, sandals, high heels and flip-flops are made for walking too.

      Shelly

TLC10522 Copyright © Christine Boardman Moen

Using Dramatic Action

1. The huge reptile with its long tail surfaces and glides quickly toward you. As it closes in on you and opens its huge jaws, you ask yourself: Is that an alligator or a crocodile?
(Paragraph Developed with Comparison-Contrast, page 64)

2. Eighth-graders are scurrying through books trying to find just the right topic for science fair! Will they find the right one in time?

Satara

Using a Fact, Statistics or Interesting Detail

1. According to the Consumer Product Safety Commission's 2002 report, nearly four million sports-related injuries requiring a doctor's visit were reported in children ages 5-16.
(Paragraph Developed with Problem-Solution, page 56)

2. Many magic tricks that are performed on stage aren't magic tricks at all. They are science.

Nathan

Personal Experience or Opinion

1. Going to the doctor and getting a shot isn't much fun. In fact, I hate getting shots of any kind.
(Paragraph Developed with Reasons, page 49)

2. There are so many different science fair topics that are interesting to me, and it's driving me crazy! So many topics with so very little time to choose!

Alyssa

As you may have noticed, I encourage students to write attention-getters that are two sentences. A two-sentence attention-getter for an informational text paragraph is a reasonable expectation.

However, although I instruct students to think about what kind of attention-getter they wish to use to open their paragraph, *it's not the first thing they write*. The very first thing students write for their paragraph is their topic sentence.

Topic Sentences in the Informational Text Paragraph

The topic sentence in each Puzzle Paragraph appears directly after the attention-getter. Placed here, the topic sentence provides the writer with a framework for his or her paragraph while it serves to signal to the reader what information he or she can expect to find while reading the paragraph.

- Without a clear topic sentence, both the writer and the reader are left directionless.

- Without a clear topic sentence, students too often veer off topic and include extraneous information or write "around" a topic without ever addressing it.

It's important to note that the topic sentence does not always appear at the beginning of all types of informational text. However, Puzzle Paragraphs are intended to be easy-to-use for teachers and easy-to-learn for students. The issue of alternative placements of topic sentences can be addressed in other readers' and writers' workshops once students learn the basics of reading and writing various kinds of informational texts.

The writer uses different kinds of topic sentences depending upon the type of paragraph he or she is writing. Explanations and examples of different topic sentences for each of the 10 Puzzle Paragraphs follow.

Types and Examples of Topic Sentences

Examples

The topic sentence in a paragraph developed with examples should state the three examples being discussed in the paragraph.

> Three towers that qualify in the tall, taller and tallest categories are the Petronas Towers, the Sears Tower and the KTHI TV Tower.

Facts

The topic sentence in a paragraph developed with facts should state the specific topic being discussed in the paragraph.

> The buffalo nickel is a small but interesting part of American history.

Reasons

The topic sentence in a paragraph developed with reasons should explain that specific reasons will be offered in the paragraph related to the topic.

> A bully can be big or small or a girl or a boy, but the reasons why someone is a bully are usually the same.

TLC10522 Copyright © Christine Boardman Moen

Cause-Effect

The topic sentence in a paragraph developed with cause-effect should briefly state the cause-effect relationship that will be discussed in the paragraph.

Acid rain, which is any type of precipitation that contains such acids as sulfuric acid and nitric acid, is caused by pollution and affects people and their environments around the world.

Problem-Solution

The topic sentence in a paragraph developed with problem-solution should briefly state the problem-solution relationship that will be discussed in the paragraph.

Although the number of young people being injured while participating in sports is a serious problem, the number of injuries can be reduced through practical means.

Comparison-Contrast

The topic sentence in a paragraph developed with comparison-contrast should introduce the topic or topics being compared and contrasted and state that similarities and differences exist between the two topics.

The African and the Asian elephant are the two species of elephants living today, and they are similar and different.

List

In the paragraph developed with a list, the topic sentence should state the topic which will be described in the paragraph through a list of information.

Throughout the ages, there have been inventions that have changed the world.

Definition

In the paragraph developed with definitions, the topic sentence is a question stated in the form of "What is . . . ?" After the question is asked, the remaining sentences in the paragraph answer the question.

What, then, is freedom?

Sequence

In the paragraph developed with sequencing, the topic sentence should briefly state the event whose sequence will be described in the paragraph.

Before astronauts could walk on the moon, they had to get there, and getting to the moon took place in several stages.

How-To Steps

The topic sentence in a paragraph developed with how-to steps should state the topic which will be explained in a series of steps.

Making friends can be as easy as A-B-C.

Concluding Sentences in the Informational Text Paragraph

There are many ways to conclude a paragraph, including making a summarizing statement, stating an opinion or offering one final detail. In addition, students can write a "circle back," whereby they return to their attention-getter or topic sentence and connect their concluding sentence to either in some way. Explanations and examples of the four different types of concluding sentences are provided here.

Types and Examples of Concluding Sentences

Summarizing

A summarizing statement can be a restatement of the paragraph's main ideas.

> Consequently, proper conditioning, proper eating and wearing the right protective equipment can help student athletes stay injury-free and stay in the competition.

> (Paragraph Developed with Problem-Solution, page 56)

One Final Detail

This concluding sentence adds a final detail that relates to all of the paragraph's main ideas.

> In other words, the Petronas Towers and the Sears Tower are a little over $1/4$ of a mile high while the KTHI TV Tower is between $1/4$ and $1/2$ mile high.

> (Paragraph Developed with Examples, page 36)

Opinion

This concluding sentence states an observation or opinion of the writer.

> Regardless of its species, elephants are distinct creatures of the earth.

> (Paragraph Developed with Comparison-Contrast, page 61)

Circle Back

Using the "circle back" statement requires that the concluding sentence reflect the introductory attention-getter or topic sentence in some way.

> Attention-Getter: "Necessity is the mother of invention" or so the saying goes. This necessity combined with people's natural curiosity resulted in inventions as simple as the raft and as complicated as the rocket.

> Circle Back: Just as curiosity and necessity helped bring about the inventions of the past, curiosity and necessity will lead to even more inventions in the future.

> (Paragraph Developed with a List, page 72)

TLC10522 Copyright © Christine Boardman Moen

Point of View

I use a football, three small signs, three note cards and three volunteers to teach point of view.

- Student A wears a sign that reads "First-Person POV(I)."
- Student B wears a sign that reads "Second-Person POV(You)."
- Student C wears a sign that reads "Third-Person POV(It)."

Each student is given a note card. The information on each student's note card is explained below.

1. First I hand the football to Student A, and he or she steps forward and reads his or her note card: "I am the quarterback. As the quarterback, I announce the plays in the huddle. I also pass the ball to a receiver, and I hand off the ball to a runner."

2. Student A hands the football to Student B, who steps forward and reads from his or her card: "If you are the quarterback, you have to announce the plays in the huddle. You also have to pass the ball to a receiver, and you have to hand off the ball to a runner."

3. Student B hands the football to Student C, who reads from his or her card: "Every team in football has a quarterback. The quarterback announces the plays in the huddle. He also passes the ball to a receiver, and he hands off the ball to a runner."

4. After this demonstration, I distribute the sentences to all students, and as a group we discuss what it means to write using different points of view.

Types and Examples of Point of View

First-Person Point of View

"I am the quarterback. As the quarterback, I announce the plays in the huddle. I also pass the ball to a receiver, and I hand off the ball to a runner."

Second-Person Point of View

"If you are the quarterback, you have to announce the plays in the huddle. You also have to pass the ball to a receiver, and you have to hand off the ball to a runner."

Third-Person Point of View

Every team in football has a quarterback. The quarterback announces the plays in the huddle. He also passes the ball to a receiver, and he hands off the ball to a runner."

5. I share different pieces of writing that are written using different points of view, and we discuss why each point of view is appropriate for each piece. I use personal essays from magazines as examples of first-person point of view and self-help articles from teen magazines as examples of second-person point of view. I use newspaper stories as examples of third-person point of view.

Figure 5

Second-Person Point of View

If you want to make friends and influence people, you should wear a smile and have a positive attitude.

Rewritten in Third-Person Point of View

Wearing a smile and having a positive attitude are helpful ways to make friends and influence people.

A lot of rules about maintaining a consistent point of view have been broken by writers and editors in recent years.

- This is good because it allows flexibility and creates interest.
- It is also bad because it can be confusing to students who are trying to use authentic texts as models for their writing.

Inexperienced as well as struggling writers often need consistent models to follow, and having too many choices and too many variables can be confusing.

6. For additional practice, I give students a piece of text written in one point of view and instruct them to convert it into a different point of view, as described in Figure 5.

With this said, I assist students in choosing the appropriate point of view for the subject of their informational text paragraph, and I ask them to maintain that point of view throughout their paragraph. Sometimes using an occasional second person "you" in a third-person point of view paragraph can add variety and interest, and students certainly should know that that is acceptable. At the same time, a writer may want to break the invisible wall between himself or herself and speak directly to the reader using "I." The most important thing about point of view is that students keep their readers in mind when they write.

TLC10522 Copyright © Christine Boardman Moen

Transitions and Signal Words

Transitions and signal words are the same thing. Writers use transitions to move smoothly from one idea to the next. Readers look for signal words to tell them when writers move from one idea to the next. Consequently, transitions and signal words need to be included as topics in readers' and writers' workshops.

The list of transitions and signal words below is a combination of many lists that I've used and combined over the years. In fact, I've combined and refined this list so much that I am no longer able to attribute any specific portion of the list to a specific author. The following list is one which my students keep in their writers' workshop folders.

Types and Examples of Transitions and Signal Words

To show cause and effect	To compare	To contrast	To add information to examples, reasons, facts, lists
accordingly	alike	although	additionally
as a result	also	but	again
because	as	despite	along with
consequently	as well as	different from	also
due to	have in common	either . . . or	and
hence	in comparison	even though	another
since	in the same way	however	as well as
so	just as	in contrast	besides
then	just like	in spite of	first
therefore	like	instead	finally
thus	likewise	nevertheless	for example
when	same	on the contrary	for instance
	similarly	on the other hand	furthermore
	similar to	otherwise	in addition
		still	moreover
		unlike	next
		yet	plus
			second
			third
			too

To explain a definition

again
another kind
another way
consists of
described as
indeed
in fact
is
surely
this means
truly
without a doubt

To provide clarity

for example
for instance
in other words
put another way

To summarize

all in all
as a result
as stated previously
consequently
finally
in brief
in conclusion
in summary
lastly
so
therefore
thus

To describe a problem and a solution

although
as a result
because
consequently
first
furthermore
in fact
one cause
one solution
next
second
while

To explain a sequence

after
afterwards
as soon as
before
during
earlier
finally
first
gradually
immediately
last
lastly
later
meanwhile
next
now
previously
soon
suddenly
then
till
today
tomorrow
when

To explain how to

about
above
across
against
along
alongside
around
as soon as
before
behind
below
beneath
beside
between
beyond
by
during
far
finally
first
in front of
inside
last
lastly
near
next
now
on top of
outside
over
second
soon
then
third
throughout
till
to the left
to the right
under
until

TLC10522 Copyright © Christine Boardman Moen

In addition to providing students with a list of transitions and signal words, I also teach students in writers' workshop to achieve paragraph coherency by repeating important words within the paragraph.

- An example of this is the repetition of the words *tall, taller, tallest* in the paragraph developed with examples found on page 36.

- Another transition device I teach is to repeat a portion of a sentence. An example of this is the repetition in the paragraphs developed through definition found on page 77.

I encourage students to repeat words and sentence portions to achieve coherency and smoothness, but when they are first starting out, I encourage them to use simple transitional words and phrases.

The bigger issue at stake in writing these paragraphs is helping students write meaningful paragraphs. That's what I want students to concentrate on first. If they don't use transitions during their first draft, I help students include them in their revised drafts until the paragraphs flow smoothly.

It's like what all those best-selling business gurus say: "Get the big jobs done first." If you can help students choose wisely the information they wish to include in their paragraph, organize it so it makes sense and write the information into paragraph format, you've helped your students get the "big job done first." The transitions and smoothing out of the writing will come as the writing gets polished and as students get more writing practice.

General Guidelines

The general guidelines that follow are exactly that: general guidelines. They are provided to serve as reference points for including Puzzle Paragraphs in your readers' and writers' workshops. The way I utilize Puzzle Paragraphs in my classroom may not fit with what you do in your classroom, so you are encouraged to make any adjustments necessary to meet your needs and the needs of your students.

Readers' Workshop: Day 1

1. Reading Aloud

1. Distribute a copy of the sample paragraph.

2. Introduce unfamiliar words in the paragraph.

3. Read the paragraph aloud. Suggested ways to read aloud the paragraph:

   - Students perform the paragraph as a nonfiction readers' theater. (This requires that you prepare the scripts ahead of time by highlighting each reader's lines.)

   - Teacher and students alternate reading sentences aloud. The teacher reads aloud a sentence then calls on a student to read aloud the next sentence. The teacher reads aloud the following sentence and then calls on another student to read aloud the next sentence. This continues until the entire paragraph has been read aloud.

   - Students buddy read with each other as the teacher circulates the room listening to students read aloud and provides assistance as needed.

   - A student begins by reading a sentence aloud and then calls on another student to read aloud who in turn calls on another student to read aloud. This continues until the entire paragraph has been read aloud.

2. Deconstructing the Paragraph

1. Give each student a copy of the paragraph's graphic organizer.

2. Students reconstruct the paragraph onto the graphic organizer. Suggested ways for students to complete the graphic organizer:

   - As students provide the appropriate information for each section of the organizer, the teacher records sentences onto an overhead transparency made from the graphic organizer Students copy onto their own organizers what the teacher writes down.

   - Students circle the different parts in the paragraph and label each part using the headings from the graphic organizer.

   - Students work in pairs and use different colored highlighters to highlight the different parts of the paragraph. For example, orange can be used to highlight the attention-getter, yellow the topic sentence, blue for the examples, pink for the details and green for the wrap-up.

   - Each student records the sentences onto his or her graphic organizer as the teacher circulates the room.

TLC10522 Copyright © Christine Boardman Moen

3. Checking for Understanding

As students reconstruct the paragraph onto the organizer, the teacher checks for understanding.

1. Teacher circulates the room asking students to explain their thinking for the arrangement of the ideas on their graphic organizer. For example, the teacher asks, "What clue(s) in the text led you to decide to arrange the sentences in this order?" or "How do you know this sentence belongs here and not some other place?"

2. When students are done reconstructing their paragraphs, the teacher either distributes copies of the completed graphic organizer or displays the completed organizer on the overhead.

3. Students check their organizers and make any corrections.

4. Choice Reading

1. Students preview the informational texts and sources gathered for this type of Puzzle Paragraph.

2. Students select a text from those offered and read independently for an allotted time.

Or

SSR: Students read their core book, a book they've chosen for independent reading, or a book they've selected for literature circles.

5. Responding to Puzzle Paragraph Reading

At this point, students respond to the reading that they did as part of the Puzzle Paragraph activity. Students are offered the following prompts and write a response to one, either in a journal or log. For a very quick check, I have students write a response on sticky notes that I categorize as I put them up on the board while we discuss them.

- I learned that this type of paragraph is organized . . . .
- With this type of paragraph, I am confused or unsure of . . . .
- This type of paragraph makes sense to me because . . . .

Readers' Workshop: Day 2

1. Putting Together the Puzzle Paragraph

1. Duplicate the Puzzle Paragraph pages.

2. Cut apart the sentence strips.

3. Put one strip of each sentence of the paragraph into a paper bag, or paper clip the set of strips together, so that each student who receives a bag or set of strips gets an entire paragraph.

4. Students reconstruct the paragraph by putting the strips in order. (Students can refer to the graphic organizer they received on Day 1.) The teacher circulates the room.

5. Ways to differentiate this include:
   - Working in pairs
   - Providing students with the beginning, middle and ending sentences
   - Omitting the attention-getter sentences

2. Checking for Understanding

As students put together their Puzzle Paragraphs, the teacher checks for understanding.

1. Teacher circulates the room asking students to explain their thinking for the arrangement of the sentences in their paragraph. For example, the teacher asks, "What clue(s) led you to decide to arrange the sentences in this order?" or "How did you know this sentence belonged here and not some other place?"

2. Students can check their reconstructed paragraphs for accuracy by doing one of the following:
   - Working in small groups, students read each other's paragraphs and make corrections.
   - Individually checking their paragraph against a copy of the reconstructed paragraph.
   - Reconstructing the paragraph using sentence strips reproduced on overhead transparency sheets. As students provide each sentence to reconstruct the paragraph, the teacher puts the correct strip on the overhead, or students walk up to the overhead as his or her sentence is required to correctly complete the paragraph. Students make corrections in their own paragraphs as the paragraph on the overhead is reconstructed.

3. Strips are collected to be used again.

TLC10522 Copyright © Christine Boardman Moen

3. Choice Reading

Students select from the informational texts and sources gathered for this type of paragraph and read independently for an allotted time. (This is the same as in Day 1. However, students should complete their previewing and settle on a text to read.)

Or

SSR: Students read independently for an allotted time from either their core book or choice book from their text set.

4. Responding to the Reading

Once again students are asked to respond to the reading that they did as part of the Puzzle Paragraph activity. Students choose from one of the following prompts or write their own response to putting together the Puzzle Paragraph:

- I prefer the activity in which I took apart the whole paragraph and rewrote its different parts or identified its different parts using the graphic organizer because . . . .

- I prefer putting the Puzzle Paragraph pieces together because . . .

- The easy part of putting together the paragraph was . . . because . . . .

- The difficult part of putting together the paragraph was . . . because . . . .

Writers' Workshop

The amount of time and the number of class periods you allot for writers' workshop will depend upon the type of writing you have chosen to do with a specific type of Puzzle Paragraph.

- My Writers' Workshop begins with a mini-lesson and then students take their desks to their personal writing spots and write for 20 to 25 minutes.

- I play soft music in the background to cover noises from the hallway while I move from student to student giving assistance and checking on progress.

- I have a hanging file folder cart on wheels in which I keep students' writing folders so they don't lose their writing.

- They can choose to put finished pieces in their permanent portfolios, which travel with them to the next grade.

- I do not allow students to throw away rough drafts or notes of any writing until we have cleaning-out parties. I've found that students throw away notes and ideas too quickly unless I monitor.

- I require students to use wide-lined, loose-leaf paper; write on alternate lines so they have room to revise and edit; and to write all final drafts in ink if they are not going to word process their final drafts. (Since I have only one computer in my classroom, and access to other school computers can be difficult at times, students usually write out their paragraphs.)

Day 1

1. Give students the rubric for the type of paragraph they are writing, and answer any questions.

2. Give students the graphic organizer for the type of paragraph they are writing. Relate the organizer to the Puzzle Paragraph from the previous day's activity.

3. If students are using Lift It, Sift It, Sort It, Organize It, then use writers' workshop to work on this activity. Or have students complete their graphic organizer and write their first drafts.

Day 2

1. Begin with a brief mini-lesson based on your review of the rough drafts; organizers; and/or Lift It, Sift It, Sort It, Organize It sheets.

2. Students complete their Lift It, Sift It, Sort It, Organize It sheets and complete their graphic organizers. Or have students revise and edit their first drafts and write their final draft.

TLC10522 Copyright © Christine Boardman Moen

Day 3

1. Students share their writing. Or students write their first drafts. Suggested ways for students to share their writing:

- Students exchange with another student who silently reads the paragraph, then exchanges with another student and so forth. (Students usually read four or five paragraphs during this activity.)

- Students gather in small groups, each student reads his or her paragraph aloud, and students comment.

- Students circle-up and create an inner circle and an outer circle. In this way students form pairs. Students read aloud their paragraph to each other and comment on each other's paragraphs. When time is up, one circle of students moves so new pairs are formed, and the process repeats itself. (Students usually read aloud their paragraph four or five times.)

2. I often conclude the workshop with a critique. I get a student's permission prior to the class meeting to make an overhead transparency copy of his or her paragraph. I display the paragraph and ask students to deconstruct it like they did the first day in writers' workshop. Students identify the attention-getter, examples, transitions and so forth. We also note the student's word choice and voice. In other words, students identify why the paragraph is well written.

Day 4

If students used Lift It, Sift, It, Sort It, Organize It:

1. Begin with a mini-lesson based on your review of the rough drafts.

2. Students revise and edit their first drafts and write their final drafts.

Day 5

If students used Lift It, Sift, It, Sort It, Organize It:

Students share as described on Day 3.

Assessing the Paragraphs and Publishing Student Work

Assessing the Paragraphs

1. Students gather all of their rough drafts, organizers and Lift It sheets along with the grading rubric and final draft of their paragraph.

2. They staple together all of this information. The final draft of the paragraph appears first in the packet and the grading rubric is the last page of the packet.

3. I read the final draft and assess it according to the rubric. I often refer to first drafts to see what types of editing and revising the student attempted and completed.

Publishing Student Work

I usually do not take Puzzle Paragraphs to the publishing stage because my students do a significant amount of other writing that is displayed and read by others. After all, my primary objective in using Puzzle Paragraphs is to help students recognize and utilize structure and organization in their expository reading and writing by engaging in activities that provide consistent, easy-to-understand and easy-to-follow informational texts.

TLC10522 Copyright © Christine Boardman Moen

Final Thoughts

By now you are anxious to get to the paragraphs and begin planning how you are going to use Puzzle Paragraphs. Before you begin, I offer these final thoughts based on my own experience:

1. Carefully look through your curricula and see where Puzzle Paragraphs will benefit students. You do not have to use all 10 paragraphs nor introduce them to students in any specific order. However, it will be necessary to connect your readers' and writers' workshops by first introducing a Puzzle Paragraph in readers' workshop and then following up with writing that type of paragraph in writers' workshop. In this way reading will inform writing, and writing will inform reading.

2. Take stock of the informational texts in your classroom and school library. Having a variety of up-to-date books is useful; however, you don't need a set of expensive nonfiction books in order to use Puzzle Paragraphs. Instead, load up a library cart of single copies of books that cover three to five different topics of interest to students, and park the cart in your classroom.

A note about book selection: When selecting books, be sure to choose books students are able to read. (This is especially important for struggling readers!) Include picture books written with older readers in mind. They often provide the necessary text features that struggling readers need and that middle school students crave to keep them focused and interested.

3. Newspapers, magazines and Web sites can also be sources of information for Puzzle Paragraphs. These are especially appropriate for struggling readers.

4. Look for opportunities to use Puzzle Paragraphs with reading and writing that you are already doing in your workshops.

   • For example, I mentioned earlier that my students read *The Outsiders* by S.E. Hinton and watched the movie of the same title by Francis Ford Coppola. This provided the perfect opportunity for students to write a comparison-contrast paragraph.

   • Another example is when students wrote a list paragraph after listening to my read-aloud of Ron Kortege's *Shakespeare Bats Clean-Up*. Students wrote a paragraph from the notes they took that described the variety of poems the author used while telling the story of an athlete who is confined to bed and writes poetry while recuperating from mononucleosis.

5. Keep an on-going list of possible topics to use with each of the 10 different Puzzle Paragraph types. Use this list for book selection and to help students who struggle with choosing a topic.

Paragraph Developed with Examples

Tall, taller, tallest. When it comes to the world's towers, some are tall, others are taller and a very few are the tallest of all. Three towers that qualify in the tall, taller and tallest categories are the Petronas Towers, the Sears Tower and the KTHI TV Tower. In the tall category are the Petronas Towers in Kuala Lumpur, Malaysia. Designed by Cesar Pelli and completed in 1998, the towers measure 1,483 feet or 452 meters. Next comes the Sears Tower in Chicago, Illinois, measuring 1,518 feet or 463 meters. The Sears Tower is 456 feet taller than the famous Eiffel Tower, which is located in Paris, France. However, the tallest tower in the world is located in North Dakota. The TV tower for station KTHI is 2,063 feet or 629 meters tall. In other words, the Petronas Towers and the Sears Tower are a little over 1/4 of a mile high while the KTHI TV Tower is between 1/4 and 1/2 mile high.

TLC10522 Copyright © Christine Boardman Moen

Graphic Organizer for Paragraph Developed with Examples:

Towers

Attention-Getter: (single words)

Tall, taller, tallest. When it comes to the world's towers, some are tall, others are taller and a very few are the tallest of all.

Topic Sentence:

Three towers that qualify in the tall, taller and tallest categories are the Petronas Towers, the Sears Tower and the KTHI TV Tower.

Example 1:

Petronas Towers in Kuala Lumpur, Malaysia

Detail:

Designed by Cesar Pelli in 1998
Measures 1,483 feet or 452 meters

Example 2:

Sears Tower in Chicago, Illinois, at 1,518 feet or 463 meters

Detail:

Measures 456 feet taller than the Eiffel Tower in Paris, France

Example 3:

KTHI is tallest tower and is located in North Dakota

Detail:

Measures 2,063 feet or 629 meters

Wrap-Up:

In other words, the Petronas Towers and the Sears Tower are are a little over $1/4$ of a mile high while the KTHI TV Tower is between $1/4$ and $1/2$ mile high.

Transitions and Signal Words:

in the tall category
next
however
in other words

Graphic Organizer for
Paragraph Developed with Examples

Attention-Getter:

Topic Sentence:

Example 1:

    Detail:

Example 2:

    Detail:

Example 3:

    Detail:

Wrap-Up:

Transitions and
Signal Words:

TLC10522 Copyright © Christine Boardman Moen

Puzzle Paragraph: Examples

If your coach BENCHED you during the middle of a game, would you be BUMMED? Most likely, yes!

American slang words and expressions can describe just about anything including people's emotions, people themselves and even making and eating food.

For example, many slang words and expressions describe people's emotions or how they feel.

People who get angry or upset are said to be "bent out of shape" or "stressed."

Slang words can also be used to describe people themselves.

For instance, you may be called a "goof-ball" if you like to act silly or a "klutz" if you're clumsy.

In addition, slang can be used to describe making and eating food.

Perhaps one time you might have "nuked," or cooked, a quick snack in a microwave and then sat and "chowed down," or ate it quickly, with great enjoyment.

Slang words and expressions come in and out of everyday language even when you may be "veging out"!

Grading Rubric:
Paragraph Developed with Examples

Name _____   Date _____

5—Outstanding   4—Very Good   3—Good   2—Needs Improvement   1—Poor Effort

_____ **Attention-getter** is effective and is modeled after one of the following types:

_____ question   _____ quotation

_____ single word   _____ dramatic action

_____ fact, statistic, interesting detail   _____ personal experience/opinion

_____ **Topic sentence** is clear and identifies the three ideas to be developed within the paragraph.

_____ The **body** of the paragraph contains the following well-written sentences:

_____ Example 1   _____ Example 2   _____ Example 3

_____ Detail 1   _____ Detail 2   _____ Detail 3

_____ There is a **wrap-up sentence** that concludes the paragraph.

_____ **Transitions and signal words** are used effectively.

Teacher Comments

What You've Done Very Well: _____

_____

_____

What You Need to Improve: _____

_____

_____

TLC10522 Copyright © Christine Boardman Moen

Paragraph Developed with Facts

". . . a wave of the rider's hand . . . and man and horse burst past . . . and go swinging away like a belated fragment of a storm." Author Mark Twain used these words in 1861 to describe a Pony Express rider who rode past the stagecoach Twain was traveling on through Nevada. Though short-lived, the Pony Express remains a remarkable part of American history. The Pony Express was established on April 3, 1860, and was in operation for less than 19 months. Its purpose was to provide speedy mail delivery between St. Joseph, Missouri, and Sacramento, California. Because the route was nearly 2,000 miles and took riders 10 days to cover, the Pony Express operated more than 150 station houses, which were located 5 to 20 miles apart. In total, about 180 riders rode during the year and a half the Pony Express operated. They were paid a salary of $25.00 per week. The Pony Express had a brief, glorious history, but some of its riders went on to become famous. One such rider was William "Buffalo Bill" Cody. Like "Buffalo Bill" himself, the Pony Express will live on as a legend of the history of the American West.

Graphic Organizer for
Paragraph Developed with Facts:

Pony Express

Attention-Getter:
(quotation) "...a wave of the rider's hand ... and man and horse burst past ... and go swinging away like a belated fragment of a storm." Author Mark Twain used these words in 1861 to describe a Pony Express rider who rode past the stagecoach Twain was traveling on through Nevada.

Topic Sentence: Though short-lived, the Pony Express remains a remarkable part of American history.

Fact 1: Established April 3, 1860, and operated less than 19 months

Fact 2: Purpose was speedy mail delivery between Missouri and California

Fact 3: Route took 10 days to cover and was nearly 2,000 miles; 150 station houses along the route 5 and 20 miles apart

Fact 4: 180 riders who earned $25.00 a week

Fact 5: William "Buffalo Bill" Cody was famous Pony Express rider

Wrap-Up: Like "Buffalo Bill" himself, the Pony Express will live on as a legend of the history of the American West.

Transitions and Signal Words:
though short-lived
because
in total
like "Buffalo Bill" himself

TLC10522 Copyright © Christine Boardman Moen

Graphic Organizer for
Paragraph Developed with Facts

Attention-Getter:

Topic Sentence:

Fact 1:

Fact 2:

Fact 3:

Fact 4:

Fact 5:

Wrap-Up:

Transitions and
Signal Words:

Puzzle Paragraph: Facts

When is a nickel worth more than five cents? When it's a 1913 mint-condition buffalo nickel, estimated to be worth thousands of dollars.

The buffalo nickel is a small but interesting part of American history.

To begin with, the buffalo nickel, which was first minted on February 17, 1913, was designed by James Fraser, an artist and sculptor who grew up in the Dakota Territory.

The face on the coin is of an American Indian chief and is actually a combination of the facial features of three chiefs: Two Moons, Iron Trail and Big Tree, who visited New York City and posed for James.

On the other side of the coin is the buffalo, which is actually an American bison whose model was Black Diamond, a bison that lived at the Central Park Zoo in New York City.

Although the buffalo nickel became very popular once it was minted and distributed, some business leaders initially objected to it because it didn't fit into their machines' coin slots.

However, the director of the Mint, George Roberts, concluded that the design of the coin should remain the same, and the design of the machines should be changed.

Consequently, James Fraser's buffalo nickel stayed in circulation for 25 years and remains a tribute to the American bison and the American Indian.

TLC10522 Copyright © Christine Boardman Moen

Grading Rubric:
Paragraph Developed with Facts

Name _____   Date _____

5—Outstanding   4—Very Good   3—Good   2—Needs Improvement   1—Poor Effort

_____ **Attention-getter** is effective and is modeled after one of the following types:

_____ question   _____ quotation

_____ single word   _____ dramatic action

_____ fact, statistic, interesting detail   _____ personal experience/opinion

_____ **Topic sentence** is clear and specifically states the topic discussed in the paragraph.

_____ The **body** of the paragraph contains five or more well-written sentences:

_____ Fact 1   _____ Fact 2   _____ Fact 3   _____ Fact 4

_____ Fact 5   _____ Fact 6   _____ Fact 7

_____ There is a **wrap-up** sentence that concludes the paragraph.

_____ **Transitions and signal words** are used effectively.

Teacher Comments
What You've Done Very Well: _____

_____

_____

What You Need to Improve: _____

_____

_____

TLC10522 Copyright © Christine Boardman Moen

Paragraph Developed with Reasons

He threatens to "mess you up" as his hand forms a fist, and he draws back his arm for the punch. This is a bully in action. A bully can be big or small or a girl or a boy, but the reasons why someone is a bully are usually the same. First, bullies become bullies because they often have been mistreated themselves, usually by a family member. As a result, bullies become bullies to make themselves feel powerful. Also, most bullies are jealous of other people's achievements. Because they can't do what others do, they choose to bully the person who does something well. Finally, believe it or not, most bullies are lonely and scared. These feelings lead bullies to act tough to cover up their loneliness and fear. Understanding why bullies act the way they do can be a first step in knowing what to do when coming face-to-face with a bully.

TLC10522 Copyright © Christine Boardman Moen

Graphic Organizer for
Paragraph Developed with Reasons:

Bullies

Attention-Getter: He threatens to "mess you up" as his hand forms a fist,
(dramatic action) and he draws back his arm for the punch. This is a bully
in action.

Topic Sentence: A bully can be big or small or a girl or a boy, but the reasons why
someone is a bully are usually the same.

Reason 1: They often have been mistreated themselves.

    Detail: They seek power.

Reason 2: They are jealous of other people's achievements.

    Detail: They bully the person who is able to do what they can't do.

Reason 3: Bullies are lonely, scared people.

    Detail: They act like bullies to cover up these feelings.

Wrap-Up: Understanding why bullies act the way they do can be a first
step in knowing what to do when coming face-to-face with a bully.

Transitions and first
Signal Words: as a result
also
because
finally

Graphic Organizer for
Paragraph Developed with Reasons

Attention-Getter:

Topic Sentence:

Reason 1:

    Detail:

Reason 2:

    Detail:

Reason 3:

    Detail:

Wrap-Up:

Transitions and
Signal Words:

TLC10522 Copyright © Christine Boardman Moen

Puzzle Paragraph: Reasons

Going to the doctor and getting a shot isn't much fun. In fact, I hate getting shots of any kind.

However, many people believe that getting shots, or vaccinations as they are called, is necessary for several reasons.

First, vaccines can help prevent birth defects, mental retardation, and paralysis.

For instance, before vaccines were routine, 20,000 newborn babies each year were born with birth defects and mental retardation due to rubella (German measles), and 10,000 people were paralyzed from polio.

Secondly, vaccines can help prevent deaths due to many common diseases.

For example, before vaccines were common, nearly 4 million people contracted measles, and 3,000 of these died.

However, the most important reason why vaccines are necessary is because if people do not get vaccinated, these diseases may become common again.

In other words, should an outbreak happen, chances are that widespread epidemics would result affecting many people.

Yes, going to the doctor to get a shot isn't fun, but the alternative is even less fun.

Grading Rubric:
Paragraph Developed with Reasons

Name _____   Date _____

5—Outstanding   4—Very Good   3—Good   2—Needs Improvement   1—Poor Effort

_____ **Attention-getter** is effective and is modeled after one of the following types:

_____ question   _____ quotation

_____ single word   _____ dramatic action

_____ fact, statistic, interesting detail   _____ personal experience/opinion

_____ **Topic sentence** is clear and states that reasons related to the paragraph's topic will be provided and explained.

_____ The **body** of the paragraph contains the following well-written sentences:

_____ Reason 1   _____ Reason 2   _____ Reason 3

_____ Detail 1   _____ Detail 2   _____ Detail 3

_____ There is a **wrap-up** sentence that concludes the paragraph.

_____ **Transitions and signal words** are used effectively.

Teacher Comments

What You've Done Very Well: _____

_____

_____

What You Need to Improve: _____

_____

_____

TLC10522 Copyright © Christine Boardman Moen

Paragraph Developed with Cause-Effect

You've heard the expression "It's raining cats and dogs." What would you think, instead, if someone told you that it's raining acid? Acid rain, which is any type of precipitation that contains such acids as sulfuric acid and nitric acid, is caused by pollution and affects people and their environments around the world. The most significant cause of acid rain is the burning of coal, oil and other fossil fuels. Factories, power plants and automobiles use these types of energy sources. Once the pollutants are in the air, whether through automobile exhaust or smokestacks, the pollutants are carried by the wind and can damage lakes and forests in different parts of the country and in different parts of the world. For example, acid clouds that are created in the Midwest can travel to the Northeast as well as Canada, where acid rain can damage lakes and forest. In Europe, many forests in Germany, the Czech Republic, Slovakia and Poland have been severely damaged by acid rain. In addition, buildings and monuments that contain limestone can be damaged and appear to "melt" as a result of the effects of acid rain. The relationship between the causes and the effects of acid rain have been proven by scientists, but the question of how to stop acid rain remains to be settled.

Graphic Organizer for
Paragraph Developed with Cause-Effect:

Acid Rain

Attention-Getter:
(quotation and
question)

You've heard the expression "It's raining cats and dogs." What would you think, instead, if someone told you it's raining acid?

Topic Sentence:

Acid rain, which is any type of precipitation that contains such acids as sulfuric acid and nitric acid, is caused by pollution and affects people and their environments around the world.

Cause:

Burning of coal, oil and fossil fuels in factories, power plants and automobiles

Effects:

Pollutants carried by the wind can damage lakes and forests
Northeast, Canada harmed by acid clouds from the Midwest
Forests in Europe have been damaged by acid rain
Limestone buildings and monuments are damaged and "melt"

Wrap-Up:

The relationship between the causes and the effects of acid rain have been proven by scientists, but the question of how to stop acid rain remains to be settled.

Transitions and
Signal Words:

causes
effects
for example
in addition
as a result

TLC10522 Copyright © Christine Boardman Moen

Graphic Organizer for
Paragraph Developed with Cause-Effect

Attention-Getter:

Topic Sentence:

Cause(s):

Effect(s):

Wrap-Up:

Transitions and
Signal Words:

Puzzle Paragraph: Cause-Effect

Black potatoes. They rotted in the fields leaving millions of Irish hungry and homeless.

The great Irish Potato Famine, which lasted from 1845 to 1850, was caused by a simple fungus, but the effects of the fungus that caused the famine were felt by millions of people.

First, the potato was the single most important food source for millions of poor Irish farm laborers. When the potato crops failed, the laborers could not feed themselves.

As a result, the laborers could not pay the rents due on the small parcels of land on which they lived.

Consequently, landlords who owned the land took away the laborers' livestock and grain crops to cover the rent payments.

Because the famine lasted several years, people were left homeless and hungry. In fact, a million people died as a result of disease and starvation during the famine.

Because so many were left homeless and hungry, 2 million people emigrated from Ireland looking for a better way of life.

One and a half million of these people came to the United States.

Due to the Irish Potato Famine, millions of people lost their lives and had to leave their homeland.

TLC10522 Copyright © Christine Boardman Moen

Grading Rubric:
Paragraph Developed with Cause-Effect

Name _____ Date _____

5—Outstanding   4—Very Good   3—Good   2—Needs Improvement   1—Poor Effort

_____ **Attention-getter** is effective and is modeled after one of the following types:

_____ question   _____ quotation

_____ single word   _____ dramatic action

_____ fact, statistic, interesting detail   _____ personal experience/opinion

_____ **Topic sentence** is clear and states the cause-effect relationship that will be developed in the paragraph.

_____ The **body** of the paragraph contains well-written sentences in two areas:

_____ Cause(s)   _____ Effect(s)

_____ There is a **wrap-up** sentence that concludes the paragraph.

_____ **Transitions and signal words** are used effectively.

Teacher Comments

What You've Done Very Well: _____

_____

_____

What You Need to Improve: _____

_____

_____

Paragraph Developed with Problem-Solution

According to the Consumer Product Safety Commission's 2002 report, nearly 4 million sports-related injuries requiring a doctor's visit were reported in children ages 5 to 16. As large as this number may be, the true number of sports-related injuries in young people is probably much higher. The Commission estimates that an additional 8 million young athletes injure themselves but do not seek medical treatment. Although the number of young people being injured while participating in sports is a serious problem, the number of injuries can be reduced through practical means. First, it's important to understand that most of the sports-related injuries occur in sports that require a lot of running. These sports include baseball, football, softball, basketball and soccer. In addition, the most common injuries involve the athlete's legs, knees, arms and shoulders, while some of the most serious injuries involve the player's head, neck and back. Although accidents and injuries will happen when young people play sports, there are practical things student athletes can do to prevent injuries or reduce the seriousness of injuries. One thing student athletes can do is condition their bodies so they are in the best possible shape to play their particular sport. Secondly, student athletes should always wear the protective equipment made for their sport and wear each piece of equipment correctly. One final thing student athletes can do to protect themselves from injuries is to eat healthy so they are burning the right "fuel" whether they are conditioning or playing. Consequently, proper conditioning, proper eating and wearing the right protective equipment can help student athletes stay injury-free and stay in the competition.

TLC10522 Copyright © Christine Boardman Moen

Graphic Organizer for Paragraph Developed with Problem-Solution:

Sports-Related Injuries

Attention-Getter:
(statistics)

According to the Consumer Product Safety Commission's 2002 report, nearly 4 million sports-related injuries requiring a doctor's visit were reported in children ages 5 to 16. As large as this number may be, the true number of sports-related injuries in young people is probably much higher. The Commission estimates that an additional 8 million young athletes injure themselves but do not seek medical treatment.

Topic Sentence:

Although the number of young people being injured while participating in sports is a serious problem, the number of injuries can be reduced through practical means.

Problem:

Most sports-related injuries occur in sports that involve a lot of running. These sports include baseball, football, softball, basketball and soccer. The most common injuries occur to the legs, knees, arms and shoulders. The most serious injuries occur to the head, neck and back.

Solution:

Athletes should condition their bodies before playing.
Athletes should always wear protective equipment.
Athletes should eat properly.

Wrap-Up:

Consequently, proper conditioning, proper eating and wearing the right protective equipment can help student athletes stay injury-free and stay in the competition.

Transitions and Signal Words:

although
first
in addition
one thing
secondly
one final thing
consequently

Graphic Organizer for Paragraph Developed with Problem-Solution

Attention-Getter:

Topic Sentence:

Problem:

Solution:

Wrap-Up:

Transitions and
Signal Words:

TLC10522 Copyright © Christine Boardman Moen

Puzzle Paragraph: Problem-Solution

Runny nose. Sneezing. Sore throat. You've caught a cold, and you don't feel good.

Although the common cold seldom results in serious illness and injury, nevertheless, the common cold can be a serious problem.

One reason the common cold is a serious problem is because it is so common. In fact, according to the National Institute of Allergy and Infectious Diseases, Americans catch 1 billion colds each year.

Adults average up to four colds each year while children develop almost 10 colds each year.

With moms and dads getting colds and staying home from work to take care of themselves or staying home to take care of their children, work days are missed.

In fact, it's estimated that lost work days due to colds cost the American economy around $5 billion!

While the cure for the common cold is not currently available and may never be successfully developed, the solution for the common cold is a combination of common sense, old-fashioned wisdom and modern medicine.

First, the best way to fight the common cold is to prevent yourself from getting one in the first place. This can be done by simply washing your hands frequently.

By washing your hands often, you'll remove the germs that cause colds so those germs can't get into your body when you rub your eye or eat your food.

A second way to avoid a cold is to eat nutritious foods and get enough rest. Doctors, and probably grandmothers, have been giving this advice for as long as the common cold has been around.

Finally, modern medicine can't help prevent your cold or cure your cold, but some medicines such as acetaminophen and decongestants can help reduce your fever and stop your runny nose.

Nobody enjoys getting a cold, so the next time people around you start coughing and sneezing, remember to take action so you are part of the solution before you become part of the problem.

Grading Rubric: Paragraph Developed with Problem-Solution

Name _____   Date _____

5—Outstanding   4—Very Good   3—Good   2—Needs Improvement   1—Poor Effort

_____ **Attention-getter** is effective and is modeled after one of the following types:

_____ question   _____ quotation

_____ single word   _____ dramatic action

_____ fact, statistic, interesting detail   _____ personal experience/opinion

_____ The **topic sentence** is clear and states the problem-solution relationship that will be developed in the paragraph.

_____ The **body** of the paragraph contains well-written sentences in two areas:

_____ problem(s)   _____ solution(s)

_____ There is a **wrap-up** sentence that concludes the paragraph.

_____ **Transitions and signal words** are used effectively.

Teacher Comments
What You've Done Very Well: _____

_____

_____

What You Need to Improve: _____

_____

_____

TLC10522 Copyright © Christine Boardman Moen

Paragraph Developed with Comparison-Contrast (One-to-One)

What mammal, besides human beings, baby-sits an other's children, risks its life to save a friend, and cares for sick relatives? The answer is the world's biggest land animal: the elephant. The African and the Asian elephant are the two species of elephants living today, and they are similar and different. First, both species are similar because they are very large animals with floppy ears, long trunks and ivory tusks. But there are differences between the two elephants in these features as well. For instance, not only is the African elephant larger than the Asian elephant but its ears are much larger as well. In addition, at the end of the African elephant's trunk are two fingerlike tips, whereas there is only one such fingerlike tip at the end of the Asian elephant's trunk. One final difference between the African and Asian elephant is that male and female African elephants have tusks while only male Asian elephants have tusks. Regardless of its species, elephants are distinct creatures of the earth.

Graphic Organizer for Paragraph Developed with Comparison-Contrast
(One-to-One)

Attention-Getter:
(question)

What mammal, besides human beings, baby-sits an other's children, risks its life to save a friend, and cares for sick relatives? The answer is the world's biggest land animal: the elephant.

Topic Sentence:

The African and the Asian elephant are the two species of elephants living today, and they are similar and different.

Statement of Similarity:

Both are similar because they have floppy ears, long trunks and ivory tusks.

Contrast 1:
(ears)

African elephant is larger than Asian and has larger ears.

Contrast 2:
(trunks)

African elephant's trunk has two fingerlike tips at the end while Asian elephant has only one.

Contrast 3:
(tusks)

Both male and female African elephants have tusks while only male Asian elephants have tusks.

Wrap-Up:

Regardless of its species, elephants are distinct creatures of the earth.

Transitions and Signal Words:

first
for instance
in addition
whereas
one final difference
regardless
repetition of ears, trunks and tusks

TLC10522 Copyright © Christine Boardman Moen

Graphic Organizer for Paragraph Developed with Comparison-Contrast
(One-to-One)

Attention-Getter:

Topic Sentence:

Statement of
Similarity:

Contrast 1:

Contrast 2:

Contrast 3:

Contrast 4:
(optional)

Wrap-Up:

Transitions and
Signal Words:

LC10522 Copyright © Christine Boardman Moen

Puzzle Paragraph: Compare-Contrast
(One-to-One)

The huge reptile with its long tail surfaces and glides quickly toward you. As it closes in on you and opens its huge jaws, you ask yourself: Is that an alligator or a crocodile?

Given that scene in real life, you wouldn't care if the reptile stalking you was an American alligator or an American crocodile, but there are ways to tell the two apart.

Each reptile's facial features are similar in that each has a snout, teeth, nasal bridges and eyes, but there are differences in these features between the alligator and the crocodile.

First, the alligator's snout is wide while the crocodile's snout is narrow.

Secondly, when the alligator closes its mouth, only its top teeth show.

On the other hand, when the crocodile closes its mouth, one big, lower tooth will show on each side of its jaws.

Also, if you had time to count teeth while you were frantically swimming away, you would notice that the alligator usually has 74 to 84 teeth while the crocodile usually has 66 to 68 teeth.

In addition, the eyes and nasal bridges are areas of similarities and differences.

Both the alligator and crocodiles have eyes, but there is a distinct swelling in front of each of the crocodile's eyes, while the bony nasal bridge of the alligator is larger than a crocodile's.

Consequently, whether it's a crocodile or an alligator you come upon, you'll want to be cautious and keep your distance until you can slip carefully and quietly away.

TLC10522 Copyright © Christine Boardman Moen

Grading Rubric:
Paragraph Developed with
Comparison-Contrast (One-to-One)

Name _____ Date _____

5—Outstanding   4—Very Good   3—Good   2—Needs Improvement   1—Poor Effort

_____ **Attention-getter** is effective and is modeled after one of the following types:

_____ question   _____ quotation

_____ single word   _____ dramatic action

_____ fact, statistic, interesting detail   _____ personal experience/opinion

_____ The **topic sentence** is clear and identifies the topics to be compared and contrasted.

_____ The **statement of similarity** identifies three ways in which the topics are similar.

_____ The **body** of the paragraph contains at least three sentences that provide contrasting information.

_____ Contrast 1   _____ Contrast 2   _____ Contrast 3   _____ Contrast 4

_____ There is a **wrap-up** sentence that concludes the paragraph.

_____ **Transitions and signal words** are used effectively.

Teacher Comments
What You've Done Very Well: _____

_____

_____

What You Need to Improve: _____

_____

_____

Paragraph Developed with Comparison-Contrast: (Block Style)

Keeping current with what is happening in the world is as easy as switching on a 24-hour news network or logging onto the Internet. Despite these immediate sources of news, people continue to read newspapers and news magazines. Although both newspapers and news magazines provide readers with news, there are other similarities as well as differences between the two. To begin with, the purpose of both newspapers and news magazines is to inform the people who read each one. In addition, both newspapers and news magazines contain many of the same types of stories, such as letters to the editor, feature stories about people and sports information. Moreover, both newspapers and news magazines use advertisements to help pay the cost of publishing the newspaper or news magazine. Despite these similarities, there are significant differences between newspapers and news magazines. First, the most obvious difference is that most large newspapers are published daily while most news magazines are published weekly or monthly. Secondly, newspapers print local or regional news related to the people who live in the area in which the newspaper is published and sold. On the other hand, news magazines publish information for a more general, widespread audience. One final and very noticeable difference between newspapers and news magazines is the use of color. Many news magazines feature color photographs, maps and advertisements throughout the entire magazine. In contrast, newspapers use color to a much lesser degree because color printing costs more than black-and-white printing. Consequently, both newspapers and news magazines seek to inform readers, but they each do it in a different way.

TLC10522 Copyright © Christine Boardman Moen

Graphic Organizer for Paragraph Developed with Comparison-Contrast
(Block Style)

Attention-Getter:
(personal experience) — Keeping current with what is happening in the world is as easy as switching on a 24-hour news network or logging onto the Internet. Despite these immediate sources of news, people continue to read newspapers and news magazines.

Topic Sentence: — Although both newspapers and news magazines provide readers with news, there are other similarities as well as differences between the two.

Similarity 1: — The purpose of both is to inform people.

Similarity 2: — Both contain many of the same types of stories, such as letters to the editor, feature stories about people, and sports information.

Similarity 3: — Both use advertisements to pay for publishing costs.

Transition Sentence to Differences: — Despite these similarities, there are significant differences between newspapers and news magazines.

Difference 1: — Large newspapers are published daily while magazines are usually published weekly or monthly.

Difference 2: — Newspapers print local, regional and state news while magazines publish information for a widespread audience.

Difference 3: — Magazines usually use more color than newspapers.

Wrap-Up: — Consequently, both newspapers and news magazines seek to inform readers, but they each do it in a different way.

Transitions and Signal Words:
although
to begin with
in addition
moreover
first
secondly
on the other hand
one final and very noticeable difference
consequently

Graphic Organizer for Paragraph Developed with Comparison-Contrast
(Block Style)

Attention-Getter:

Topic Sentence:

Difference 1:

Difference 2:

Difference 3:

Transition
Sentence to
Similarities:

Similarity 1:

Similarity 2:

Similarity 3:

Wrap-Up:

Transitions and
Signal Words:

TLC10522 Copyright © Christine Boardman Moen

Graphic Organizer for Paragraph Developed with Comparison-Contrast
(Block Style)

Attention-Getter:

Topic Sentence:

Similarity 1:

Similarity 2:

Similarity 3:

Transition
Sentence to
Differences:

Difference 1:

Difference 2:

Difference 3:

Wrap-Up:

Transitions and
Signal Words:

Puzzle Paragraph:
Comparison-Contrast (Block Style)

Thomas Jefferson, the third President of the United States, believed strongly in public education. In fact, he believed so strongly that when the Northwest Territories were opened, he had land in those territories set aside for public schools so that ". . . schools, and the means of education, shall forever be preserved."

If you attended some of those public schools in the mid-1800s, you'd discover that they were alike yet different from the schools you attend today.

To begin with, if you went to school in the mid-1800s, you would probably attend a school where students of all ages and grade levels learned in one room.

In this one-room schoolhouse, girls sat on one side of the room, and boys sat on the other side.

The school year was also divided into a summer session and a winter session.

Although the schools of the mid-1800s were different in many ways from today's schools, some similarities exist.

For instance, many schools today like the schools of the mid-1800s begin the school day with either singing "The Star-Spangled Banner" or saying the Pledge of Allegiance.

Also, today students still study subjects such as reading, writing, mathematics and spelling.

However, the most important similarity between schools of the mid-1800s and the schools of today is that both hoped and continue to hope to educate its citizens to contribute and participate in American democracy.

With these similarities and differences in mind, you can only imagine the similarities and differences that will exist between today's schools and the schools of the mid-2100s.

TLC10522 Copyright © Christine Boardman Moen

Grading Rubric: Paragraph Developed with Comparison-Contrast (Block Style)

Name _____ Date _____

5—Outstanding 4—Very Good 3—Good 2—Needs Improvement 1—Poor Effort

_____ **Attention-getter** is effective and is modeled after one of the following types:

_____ question   _____ quotation

_____ single word   _____ dramatic action

_____ fact, statistic, interesting detail   _____ personal experience/opinion

_____ The **topic sentence** states the topics being compared and contrasted and acknowledges that similarities and differences exist between the two.

_____ The **body** of the paragraph contains the following well-written sentences:

_____ Similarity 1   _____ Similarity 2   _____ Similarity 3

_____ Transition sentence to differences

_____ Difference 1   _____ Difference 2   _____ Difference 3

_____ There is a **wrap-up** sentence that concludes the paragraph.

_____ **Transitions and signal words** are used effectively.

Teacher Comments
What You've Done Very Well: _____

_____

_____

What You Need to Improve: _____

_____

_____

Paragraph Developed with a List

"Necessity is the mother of invention," or so the saying goes. This necessity combined with people's natural curiosity resulted in inventions as simple as the raft and as complicated as the rocket. Throughout the ages, there have been inventions that have changed the world. Two of the earliest inventions created before 3500 B.C. were the boat and the axle. Boats allowed people to travel over water to trade and explore, while the axle allowed people to carry heavy loads and travel over land. The Metal Age, which includes the years 3500 B.C. to A.D. 1, came next, and it was during this time that writing, money and maps were developed and became more common. People used writing to record their history and to record their business deals. Money helped make buying and selling things easier, and maps made travel faster so people could conduct their business. In the following period, from A.D. 1 to 1799 which is called the Age of Discovery, two inventions helped people look at things up close and far away. The microscope enabled people to look closely at the world around them, which led to an understanding and the eventual cures of many diseases. The telescope allowed people to study the heavens to gain knowledge of Earth's place in the universe. The period between 1799 and 1887 is called the Age of Electricity and Communication, and it brought two revolutionary inventions: the internal combustion engine and the incandescent light bulb. Automobiles came into existence once the internal combustion engine was created, and the light bulb made it possible for people to live more flexible lives because their activities were not confined to the hours between sunrise and sunset. From 1887 to the present is the Age of the Atom, in which airplanes and computers have been invented. Both bring speed to life in the 21st century, where people travel frequently and information is shared almost instantly. Just as curiosity and necessity helped bring about the inventions of the past, curiosity and necessity will lead to even more inventions in the future.

TLC10522 Copyright © Christine Boardman Moen

Graphic Organizer for Paragraph Developed with a List

Attention-Getter:
(quotation)
"Necessity is the mother of invention," or so the saying goes. This necessity combined with people's natural curiosity resulted in inventions as simple as the raft and as complicated as the rocket.

Topic Sentence:
Throughout the ages, there have been inventions that have changed the world.

List Item 1:
Two of the earliest inventions were the boat and axle.

    Detail:
Boats allowed travel over water while axles allowed travel over land.

List Item 2:
Writing, money and maps were developed during the Metal Age.

    Detail:
People used writing to record history and to record business deals.
Money helped make buying and selling things easier.
Maps made travel faster.

List Item 3:
The Age of Discovery brought two important inventions.

    Detail:
Microscope enabled people to investigate diseases.
Telescope allowed people to study the heavens.

List Item 4:
The inventions of the internal combustion engine and the incandescent light bulb occurred during the Age of Electricity and Communication.

    Detail:
Automobiles were invented.
The light bulb allowed people to live more flexible lives.

List Item 5:
The Age of the Atom brought airplanes and computers.

    Detail:
Both inventions brought speed of travel and information.

Wrap-Up:
Just as curiosity and necessity helped bring about the inventions of the past, curiosity and necessity will lead to even more inventions in the future.

Transitions and Signal Words:
throughout the ages
two of the earliest inventions
next
not only . . . but also
in the following
from . . . to
just as

Graphic Organizer for
Paragraph Developed with a List

Attention-Getter:

Topic Sentence:

List Item 1:

    Detail:

List Item 2:

    Detail:

List Item 3:

    Detail:

List Item 4:

    Detail:

List Item 5:

    Detail:

List Item 6:
(optional)
    Detail:

List Item 7:
(optional)
    Detail:

Wrap-Up:

Transitions and
Signal Words:

TLC10522 Copyright © Christine Boardman Moen

Puzzle Paragraph: List

If you were a tourist in America today, you'd be taking photographs and mailing postcards of such tourist spots as the White House, the Empire State Building or a famous sports stadium. If you were a tourist living 2000 years ago in the eastern Mediterranean, you'd be visiting the Seven Wonders of the Ancient World.

The Seven Wonders of the Ancient World were incredible masterpieces of architecture, sculpture and engineering that ancient poets described as monuments of great beauty and grandeur.

The largest of these monuments, and the only one still in existence today, is the Great Pyramid at Giza in modern-day Egypt.

The pyramid stands nearly 500 feet tall and contains over 2 million cut-stone blocks, each one weighing between 2 and 15 tons.

While the remaining six monuments no longer exist, some believe that the Hanging Gardens of Babylon never existed at all but were instead mythical.

Nevertheless, the gardens were supposedly a vast tree-filled park built high off the ground on stone terraces within the city walls of Babylon.

Two of the ancient wonders were statues dedicated to Greek gods. First, the Colossus of Rhodes was a 110-foot-tall bronze statue of the Greek sun god, Helios.

The other statue, located at the site where the ancient Olympics took place, was a 40-foot statue of Zeus made of ivory and gold.

An additional ancient wonder was a temple while another ancient wonder was a tomb.

The Temple of Artemis was located in the city of Ephesus and was remarkable for its 127 60-foot-tall stone columns.

A mausoleum is also a tomb, and the mausoleum at Halicarnassus was the tomb of King Mausolus and his wife Artemisia.

The tomb had three parts: the bottom shaped like a rectangular podium, the middle shaped like a Greek temple and the top shaped like an Egyptian pyramid.

The final ancient wonder is called the Pharos at Alexandria, which was a giant lighthouse at the harbor of the ancient capital of Alexandria, a city founded by Alexander the Great.

The Seven Wonders of the Ancient World were spectacular and make you wonder what the seven wonders of our world will be in 2000 years.

Grading Rubric:
Paragraph Developed with a List

Name _____   Date _____

5—Outstanding   4—Very Good   3—Good   2—Needs Improvement   1—Poor Effort

_____ **Attention-getter** is effective and is modeled after one of the following types:

_____ question   _____ quotation

_____ single word   _____ dramatic action

_____ fact, statistic, interesting detail   _____ personal experience/opinion

_____ The **topic sentence** is well-written and states the topic, which will be described in the paragraph through a list of information.

_____ The **body** of the paragraph contains well-written sentences that state five to seven list items accompanied with five to seven details.

_____ List 1   _____ List 2   _____ List 3   _____ List 4
_____ Detail 1   _____ Detail 2   _____ Detail 3   _____ Detail 4

_____ List 5   _____ List 6   _____ List 7
_____ Detail 5   _____ Detail 6   _____ Detail 7

_____ There is a **wrap-up** sentence that concludes the paragraph.

_____ **Transitions and signal words** are used effectively.

Teacher Comments
What You've Done Very Well: _____

_____

_____

What You Need to Improve: _____

_____

_____

TLC10522 Copyright © Christine Boardman Moen

Paragraph Developed with Definitions

Liberty. Independence. These words are synonyms for *freedom*, something so valuable that no amount of money in the world can buy it and no amount of technology in the world can measure it. What, then, is freedom? Freedom is you being able to accomplish all that you wish without being unfairly held down or held back. Freedom is you being able to hold on to your beliefs even if they are different from other people's beliefs. Freedom is you being able to move from one place to another place, like from one city to another city, without getting permission. Freedom is you being able to say what you think and think what you want without being worried about being put in jail or being arrested. In reality, freedom is you, because only you can keep the idea of freedom alive when you act, speak and think freely and let others do so too.

Graphic Organizer for Paragraph Developed with Definitions

Attention-Getter:
(single word)

Liberty. Independence. These words are synonyms for *freedom*, something so valuable that no amount of money in the world can buy it and no amount of technology in the world can measure it.

Topic Sentence:

What, then, is freedom?

Definition 1:

Freedom is being able to accomplish what you wish without being held back or held down.

Definition 2:

Freedom is being able to hold on to your beliefs even if they are different from other people's beliefs.

Definition 3:

Freedom is being able to move about without permission.

Definition 4:

Freedom is being able to speak freely without being arrested.

Wrap-Up:

In reality, freedom is you, because only you can keep the idea of freedom alive when you act, speak and think freely and let others do so too.

Transitions and Signal Words:

what, then
freedom is
in reality

TLC10522 Copyright © Christine Boardman Moen

Graphic Organizer for
Paragraph Developed with Definitions

Attention-Getter:

Topic Sentence:

Definition 1:

Definition 2:

Definition 3:

Definition 4:

Definition 5:
(optional)

Definition 6:
(optional)

Wrap-Up:

Transitions and
Signal Words:

TLC10522 Copyright © Christine Boardman Moen

Puzzle Paragraph: Definitions

Water swirled around the firefighter's body as he struggled to rescue the frightened family while the floodwaters poured over the broken levee and into their home.   The next day, the television stations and newspapers described the firefighter's bravery and called him a hero. However, in everyday life, most acts of bravery are not dramatic rescues that take place in life-threatening situations but instead are much more ordinary.

What is bravery?

Bravery is standing up for someone when he or she is being bullied or being teased.

Bravery is telling the truth even when lying could probably keep you from being held accountable.

Bravery is forgiving someone who has hurt you in some way and accepting that person's apology.

Bravery is being persistent even when things are difficult and it would be easier just to give up.

Bravery involves all the little acts of heroism people do each day that help all of us live in harmony and with less conflict.

TLC10522 Copyright © Christine Boardman Moen

Grading Rubric: Paragraph Developed with Definitions

Name _____   Date _____

5—Outstanding   4—Very Good   3—Good   2—Needs Improvement   1—Poor Effort

_____ **Attention-getter** is effective and is modeled after one of the following types:

_____ question   _____ quotation

_____ single word   _____ dramatic action

_____ fact, statistic, interesting detail   _____ personal experience/opinion

_____ The **topic sentence** is in question form and asks "What is . . ."

_____ The **body** of the paragraph contains four to six well-written sentences that define the topic of the paragraph.

_____ Definition 1   _____ Definition 2   _____ Definition 3

_____ Definition 4   _____ Definition 5   _____ Definition 6

_____ There is a **wrap-up** sentence that concludes the paragraph.

_____ **Transitions and signal words** are used effectively.

Teacher Comments

What You've Done Very Well: _____

_____

_____

What You Need to Improve: _____

_____

_____

Paragraph Developed with Sequencing

Chances are you probably know someone who watched the first moon landing on television and listened as Neal Armstrong said, "That's one small step for man, one giant leap for mankind." The first moon landing was an historical event. However, before the astronauts could walk on the moon, they had to get there, and getting to the moon took place in several stages. First, *Apollo 11* blasted into space on July 16, 1969. Within minutes of blast-off, the astronauts began orbiting Earth, and after one-and-a-half orbits, *Apollo* and the astronauts aboard rocketed into space. While traveling through space, the astronauts moved the *Eagle* and the *Columbia* portions of the spacecraft into position so they could be used in the moon landing. Then, on the morning of the fourth day, the astronauts passed behind the moon and did what is called an "engine burn" to slow down the spacecraft so it could be drawn into the moon's gravity. Finally, on July 20, astronauts Buzz Aldrin and Neal Armstrong floated into the *Eagle* and prepared to land it on the moon. With great skill and courage, Armstrong brought the *Eagle* to rest in an area of the moon that is called the Sea of Tranquility and announced to the world, "The *Eagle* has landed." Billions of people all over the world watched the moon landing, and chances are you know one of them.

TLC10522 Copyright © Christine Boardman Moen

Graphic Organizer for Paragraph Developed with Sequencing

Attention-Getter:
(quotation-personal experience)

Chances are you probably know someone who watched the first moon landing on television and listened as Neal Armstrong said, "That's one small step for man, one giant leap for mankind." The first moon landing was an historical event.

Topic Sentence:

However, before the astronauts could walk on the moon, they had to get there, and getting to the moon took place in several stages.

Step 1:

Apollo 11 blasted into space on July 16, 1969.

Step 2:

After one-and-a-half orbits, Apollo rocketed into space.

Step 3:

Astronauts move the *Eagle* and the *Columbia* into position.

Step 4:

On the fourth day, the astronauts complete an "engine burn."

Step 5:

Buzz Aldrin and Neal Armstrong prepare the *Eagle* to land on the moon.

Step 6:

Astronauts land the *Eagle* on the moon's Sea of Tranquility and announce "The *Eagle* has landed."

Wrap-Up:

Billions of people all over the world watched the moon landing, and chances are you know one of them.

Transitions and Signal Words:

however
first
within minutes of blast-off
while
then
finally
chances are you

Graphic Organizer for Paragraph Developed with Sequencing

Attention-Getter:

Topic Sentence:

Step 1:

Step 2:

Step 3:

Step 4:

Step 5:

Step 6:

Step 7:
(optional)

Step 9:
(optional)

Step 8:
(optional)

Step 10:
(optional)

Wrap-Up:

Transitions and
Signal Words:

TLC10522 Copyright © Christine Boardman Moen

Puzzle Paragraph: Sequencing

Imagine yourself on a small, wooden ship crossing the Atlantic Ocean in the summer of 1609. Now imagine that the ship is not only struck by a hurricane, but also the boat begins to leak! If you can imagine all this and more, you are ready to learn about the real-life adventures of the people aboard the *Sea Venture*.

The adventure began on June 2, 1609, when the *Sea Venture* along with eight other ships left Plymouth, England, bound for the English colony at Jamestown, Virginia.

Sailing was smooth during June and most of July until July 23, when a storm that developed into a hurricane swept over the *Sea Venture*.

The ship began to leak, and for the next five days all people aboard bailed water, threw provisions and trunks overboard to lighten the ship, worked the sails and managed to hang on.

On July 28, the ship crashed into a reef on the northeast shore of Bermuda, and the passengers and crew rushed ashore.

Luckily the crew was able to return to the *Sea Venture* and bring ashore cargo, tools and even parts of the ship itself, including masts, sails and iron fittings. Although shipwrecked, the people aboard the *Sea Venture* found everything they needed on the island of Bermuda, including comfortable weather, plentiful food such as wild hogs, and a variety of materials to use to build shelters.

Once the people from the ship had been settled, the leaders of the voyage knew they had to send word that the people from the *Sea Venture* were alive and needed to be rescued.

Consequently, on Monday, August 28, one month after being shipwrecked, eight men set sail in a longboat to make the 600-mile voyage to Jamestown.

No rescue ship arrived, so by the end of November the leaders of the *Sea Venture* knew they would have to build new ships and rescue themselves. For the next five months, the people of the *Sea Venture* used the plentiful wood supply on Bermuda to build two ships, the *Deliverance* and the *Patience*.

Finally, they set sail from Bermuda on May 10, 1610, and arrived at the Jamestown settlement 11 days later, on May 21.

To their disappointment, the people of the *Sea Venture* discovered that most of the people of Jamestown, including those on the ships that left England in 1609, were dead due to starvation, disease and enemy attack. They also learned that the people sent from Bermuda on the longboat months earlier had never arrived in Jamestown.

The story of the shipwreck of the *Sea Venture* on Bermuda and its final arrival at the colony of Jamestown is truly remarkable adventure that most of us can only imagine.

Grading Rubric:
Paragraph Developed with Sequencing

Name _____   Date _____

5—Outstanding   4—Very Good   3—Good   2—Needs Improvement   1—Poor Effort

_____ **Attention-getter** is effective and is modeled after one of the following types:

_____ question   _____ quotation

_____ single word   _____ dramatic action

_____ fact, statistic, interesting detail   _____ personal experience/opinion

_____ The **topic sentence** states the event whose sequence will be described in the paragraph.

_____ The **body** of the paragraph contains five to 10 well-written sentences that describe an event in sequence.

_____ Step 1   _____ Step 2   _____ Step 3   _____ Step 4   _____ Step 5

_____ Step 6   _____ Step 7   _____ Step 8   _____ Step 9   _____ Step 10

_____ There is a **wrap-up** sentence that concludes the paragraph.

_____ **Transitions and signal words** are used effectively.

Teacher Comments
What You've Done Very Well: _____

_____

_____

What You Need to Improve: _____

_____

_____

TLC10522 Copyright © Christine Boardman Moen

Paragraph Developed with How-To Steps

What do a science fair project, a woodworking project and a skit for drama class have in common? They all require planning in order to complete them well. Planning is the essential key to success when it comes to completing projects of any kind. The first step in planning a project is to write a statement of exactly what you plan to do. Knowing exactly your purpose will help you stay focused and not get distracted by extra details. The next step is to list all of the materials that you will need in order to complete the project. Gathering all of your materials before you start will save you time when you actually begin completing your project. Thirdly, you need to list all of the steps you think you will need to follow in order to complete your project. Thinking through the steps you plan to follow in the order in which they should be done can help you avoid costly mistakes. The final step in your plan is to think of any problems you may encounter while completing your project and what you could do to solve those problems. You certainly can't plan for every possible problem, but you can think ahead to avoid some that may come up. Of course, planning doesn't always guarantee success, but it sure can help!

Graphic Organizer for Paragraph Developed with How-To Steps

Attention-Getter:
(question)
What do a science fair project, a woodworking project and a skit for drama class have in common? They all require planning in order to complete them well.

Topic Sentence:
Planning is the essential key to success when it comes to completing projects of any kind.

Step 1:
Write a statement of exactly what you plan to do.

Detail:
This statement will keep you focused and help you avoid distractions.

Step 2:
List all of the materials you will need.

Detail:
Having all of your materials will save you time.

Step 3:
List the steps you must follow in order to complete the project.

Detail:
Listing the steps will help you avoid costly mistakes.

Step 4:
Think of any problems you may have while doing the project.

Detail:
Having solutions before problems occur can save time.

Wrap-Up:
Of course, planning doesn't always guarantee success, but it sure can help!

Transitions and Signal Words:
the first step
the next step
thirdly
the final step
of course, planning

TLC10522 Copyright © Christine Boardman Moen

Graphic Organizer for Paragraph Developed with How-To Steps

Attention-Getter:

Topic Sentence:

Step 1:

     Detail:

Step 2:

     Detail:

Step 3:

     Detail:

Step 4:

     Detail:

Step 5:
(optional)
     Detail:

Step 6:
(optional)
     Detail:

Wrap-Up:

Transitions and
Signal Words:

TLC10522 Copyright © Christine Boardman Moen

Puzzle Paragraph: How-To Steps

Having friends to talk to and to share experiences with makes life more enjoyable. But how do you go about making friends when you move to a new school or your old friends seem to have drifted away?

Making friends can be as easy as A-B-C.

First comes A, which stands for "Ask questions."

If you want to make friends, ask other people questions so they can talk and you can learn more about them.

After you ask someone a question, you need to follow step "B." Be a good listener and really take an interest in what other people say.

"B" can also help remind you to "be" the kind of person you want to be around, and that way you will attract people who are a lot like you.

One additional thing you can do to make friends is to find something in Common with other people.

Finding something in common like music, games or sports represents step "C."

Making friends will take time, but just remember to follow your ABCs!

TLC10522 Copyright © Christine Boardman Moen

Grading Rubric:
Paragraph Developed with How-To Steps

Name _____ Date _____

5—Outstanding   4—Very Good   3—Good   2—Needs Improvement   1—Poor Effort

_____ **Attention-getter** is effective and is modeled after one of the following types:

_____ question   _____ quotation

_____ single word   _____ dramatic action

_____ fact, statistic, interesting detail   _____ personal experience/opinion

_____ The **topic sentence** states the topic that will be explained in a series of how-to steps.

_____ The **body** of the paragraph contains well-written sentences that state four to six steps accompanied by four to six details.

_____ Step 1	_____ Step 2	_____ Step 3
_____ Detail 1	_____ Detail 2	_____ Detail 3
_____ Step 4	_____ Step 5	_____ Step 6
_____ Detail 4	_____ Detail 5	_____ Detail 6

_____ There is a **wrap-up** sentence that concludes the paragraph.

_____ **Transitions and signal words** are used effectively.

Teacher Comments
What You've Done Very Well: _____

_____

_____

What You Need to Improve: _____

_____

_____

Book Lists

American Library Association Notable Children's Books
www.ala.org

Every March *Booklist*, published by the American Library Association, prints a list of notable fiction and nonfiction books for children.

International Reading Association's Children's Choices
www.reading.org/choices/

Every October, IRA publishes a list of books that receive the highest votes from children. Two additional lists published by IRA include "Teacher Choices" and "Young Adult Choices."

Notable Children's Trade Books in the Field of Social Studies
www.socialstudies.org/resources/notable/

This list appears every June in *Social Education*, published by the National Council for the Social Studies.

Orbis Pictus Award for Outstanding Nonfiction for Children
www.ncte.org/elem/orbispictus/

This list appears in the October issue of *Language Arts*, published by the National Council of Teachers of English.

Outstanding Science Trade Books for Children
www.nsta.org

This list is published each March in the journal *Science and Children*.

ALSC/Robert F. Sibert Informational Book Award
www.ala.org

This list appears in conjunction with the Newbery and Caldecott awards which are presented in late January or early February by the American Library Association.

TLC10522 Copyright © Christine Boardman Moen

Lift It, Sift It, Sort It, Organize It

Name _____   Date _____

Read It   Carefully read the article. Read it a second time. Think!

Lift It   Select important details from the article and briefly record them on the lines provided.

Sift It   Read the details you've selected and put a star or check mark by the ones you think are the most important to include in your paragraph.

Sort It   Ask yourself:
   - What does all this information add up to?
   - What does this information say about the topic?
   - What will I be trying to tell the reader with this information?

             Next, review your graphic organizer and then ask:
   - How does this information fit onto the organizer?

Organize It   After you record your information onto the organizer, ask yourself:
   - Have I recorded the information in the correct areas on the organizer?
   - Do I have enough information?
   - Do I need to return to the text and/or my notes and select even more information?

Title/author/source of your information: _____

_____

_____

Sift It   Lift It

_____   _____

_____   _____

_____   _____

_____   _____

_____   _____

_____   _____

_____   _____

_____   _____

_____   _____

_____   _____

_____   _____

_____   _____

_____   _____

_____   _____

_____   _____

_____   _____

TLC10522 Copyright © Christine Boardman Moen

Source Information Record

Name _____   Date _____

Record the source(s) of your information in the appropriate spaces below. **This sheet must be turned in to your teacher along with your completed paragraph.**

If you've taken information from a book, record information in the following spaces:
- Author's name
- Title of book
- Copyright date
- Place of publication
- Publisher's name

If you've taken information from an online newspaper, magazine or Web page, record information in the following spaces:
- Author's name or name of producer of the Web page
- Title of the magazine, newspaper or Web page
- Title of the article
- Copyright date or date Web page was updated
- Volume number if available
- Page numbers of newspaper or magazine
- Date you retrieved the information from your online source
- Web address

Name of author(s) or producer of the information: _____

_____

Title of book, magazine, newspaper or Web page: _____

Title of newspaper or magazine article: _____

Copyright date of book, magazine, newspaper and/or date Web page was updated:

_____

Volume number of newspapers or magazines if available: _____

Page numbers of book, magazine or newspaper: _____

Book's place of publication: _____

Book's publisher: _____

Date of retrieval from online source: _____

Web page or online source Web Address: _____

Transitions

Name _____   Date _____

Transitions are all about smooth moves—moving smoothly from one idea to the next so your reader isn't surprised or confused when reading the many ideas in your paragraph. In fact, you have a responsibility to your reader to keep him or her "on the right track" and moving easily through your writing.

The easiest way to help your reader is to use transitional words and/or phrases that build bridges between ideas. There are many words and expressions that can be used as transitions. Many are useful with several different types of paragraphs, while some are especially useful to specific types of paragraphs. Still other words and expressions can be used as you conclude your paragraph or when you wish to clarify an idea within your paragraph. Remember to keep this list handy as you write, revise and edit your paragraph.

To show cause and effect	To compare	To contrast	To add information to examples, reasons, facts, lists
accordingly	alike	although	additionally
as a result	also	but	again
because	as	despite	along with
consequently	as well as	different from	also
due to	have in common	either . . . or	and
hence	in comparison	even though	another
since	in the same way	however	as well as
so	just as	in contrast	besides
then	just like	in spite of	first
therefore	like	instead	finally
thus	likewise	nevertheless	for example
when	same	on the contrary	for instance
	similarly	on the other hand	furthermore
	similar to	otherwise	in addition
		still	moreover
		unlike	next
		yet	plus
			second
			third
			too

TLC10522 Copyright © Christine Boardman Moen

To explain a definition

again
another kind
another way
consists of
described as
indeed
in fact
is
surely
this means
truly
without a doubt

To provide clarity

for example
for instance
in other words
put another way

To summarize

all in all
as a result
as stated previously
consequently
finally
in brief
in conclusion
in summary
lastly
so
therefore
thus

To describe a problem and a solution

although
as a result
because
consequently
first
furthermore
in fact
one cause
one solution
next
second
while

To explain a sequence

after
afterwards
as soon as
before
during
earlier
finally
first
gradually
immediately
last
lastly
later
meanwhile
next
now
previously
soon
suddenly
then
till
today
tomorrow
when

To explain how to

about
above
across
against
along
alongside
around
as soon as
before
behind
below
beneath
beside
between
beyond
by
during
far
finally
first
in front of
inside
last
lastly
near
next
now
on top of
outside
over
second
soon
then
third
throughout
till
to the left
to the right
under
until

TLC10522 Copyright © Christine Boardman Moen

References: Professional Sources

Calkins, L.M., Montgomery, K., Santman, D. and Falk, B. (1998). *A Teacher's Guide to Standardized Reading Tests.* Portsmouth, NH: Henemann.

Flood, J., Lapp, D., and Farnan, N. (February 1986). "A Reading-Writing Procedure that Teaches Expository Paragraph Structure." *The Reading Teacher,* vol. 39, pp. 556-62.

Harvey, S. (1998). *Nonfiction Matters.* Portland, ME: Stenhouse Publishers.

Houston, G. (2004). *How Writing Works: Imposing Organizational Structure Within the Writing Process.* Boston: Pearson.

Kemper, D., Sebranek, P. and Meyer, V. (2001). *Writers Inc: A Student Handbook for Writing and Learning.* Wilmington, MA: Houghton Mifflin.

McKenzie, J. (2000). *Beyond Technology: Questioning, Research and the Information Literate School.* FNO Press.

Meyer, B.I.F. (1975). *The Organization of Prose and Its Effect on Memory.* Amsterdam: North Holland.

Moen, C.B. (2005). "Reading and Writing in the Real World." *Illinois Reading Council Journal.* Normal, IL: Illinois Reading Council.

Pappas, C.C. (1991). "Fostering Full Access to Literacy by Including Information Books." *Language Arts,* vol. 68, pp. 449-461.

Portalupi, J., and Fletcher, R. (2001). *Nonfiction Craft Lessons.* Portland, ME: Stenhouse Publishers.

Vacca, R. "Decoders to Strategic Readers." *Educational Leadership,* vol. 60(3), pp. 7-11.

Wormeli, R. (2004). *Summarization in Any Subject.* Alexandria, VA: ASCD.

Young, Righeimer, and Montbriand. (2002). *The Strategic Teaching and Reading Project: Comprehension Resource Handbook.* Naperville, IL: NCREL.

TLC10522 Copyright © Christine Boardman Moen

References: Puzzle Paragraphs

Bail, R. (1999). *One-Room School*. Boston: Houghton Mifflin.

Bartoletti, S.C. (2001). *Black Potatoes: The Story of the Great Irish Famine, 1845-1850*. Boston: Houghton Mifflin.

Britton, A. "Crocodilian Species List" Hosted by Crocodile Specialist Group. http://www.flmnh.ufl.edu. Retrieved July 24, 2005.

Children's Hospital of Philadelphia. "Vaccine Education Center" http://www.chop.edu. Retrieved July 23, 2005.

Clayton, L. (1995). *Sports Injuries*. New York: Rosen Publishing.

Curlee, L. (2002). *Seven Wonders of the Ancient World*. New York: Atheneum Books.

Fraser, M.A. (1993). *One Giant Leap*. New York: Henry Holt.

Fuchs, B. (2004). *Ride Like the Wind: A Tale of the Pony Express*. New York: Scholastic.

Johnston, M. (1996). *Dealing with Bullying*. New York: Rosen Publishing.

Karwoski, G.L. (2004). *Miracle: The True Story of the Wreck of the **Sea Venture***. Plain City, OH: Darby Creek Publishing.

Lopez, G. (1992). *Air Pollution*. Mankato, MN: Creative Education.

Mann. D. Jan. 27, 2000. "Cure for the Common Cold...The Elusive Search" http://my.webmd.com/content/Article/21/1728_54412.htm. Retrieved July 27, 2005.

Morrison, T. (2002). *The Buffalo Nickel*. Boston: Houghton Mifflin.

"Preventing Youth Sports Injuries." *USA Today Magazine*, Sept. 95, vol. 124, Issue 2604, p. 6.

Savage, A. (2003). *Famous Structures*. Chicago: Wright Group/McGraw-Hill.

Schwabacher, M. (2001). *Elephants*. New York: Marshall Cavendish.

Tomecek. S. (2003). *What a Great Idea: Inventions that Changed the World*. New York: Scholastic.

U.S. Consumer Product Safety Commission: National Injury Information Clearinghouse. http://www.nyssf.org. Retrieved July 21, 2004.

"Van Der Linde, L. (1993). *The Pony Express*. New York: New Discovery Books.

Student Example

*   3 people signed from Delaware— Thomas McKean, Caesar

____   Rodney and George Read

*   Thomas McKean held more major offices than any other

____   American of his time period (not paraphrased)

*   Lived to be 83, born in 1734 and dying in 1817

*   Married (1763) Mary Borden and had six kids (Mary died 1773)

*   Then married Sarah Armitage and had five more kids

____   Practiced law and often swayed juries with fake humor

____   Served in the legislature for more than 15 years in Delaware

____   Served in the American army and almost killed in New Jersey

____   Signed during the year 1777

____   Served as two governors, one chief Justice, president of the

____   continental congress, helped frame 2 state constitutions

*   Caesar Rodney never married but raised many relatives children

*   Born in 1728 lived to be 56 years old

*   George Read married Gertrude Ross Till

*   Born in 1733 lived to be 65 years old

*   4 people signed from Connecticut—Oliver Wolcott, Samuel

____   Huntington, William Williams, Roger Sherman

TLC10522 Copyright © Christine Boardman Moen

Student Example

Sift It	Lift It	Todd

*   Caesar's most well known deed was that he rode all night to get to Pennsylvania to vote for independence while extremely ill with cancer

*   George Read signed both the D.I. and the U.S. Constitution but signed the Constitution twice

*   Oliver Wolcott married Laura Collins and had 5 kids

*   He was born in 1726 and lived to be 71 years old

*   When the head of a felled statue of King George the III was sent to England, he took the rest home from the sight in New York and melted it to be made into bullets which were used in the British battle

*   Samuel Huntington married Martha Devotion and had no kids but raised some relatives kids

*   Samuel was born in 1731 and lived to be 64 years old

*   He is considered by some to be our nation's first president because he was president when we gained our freedom and became the Articles of the Confederation

*   William Williams married Mary Trumbull and had 3 kids

*   Born in 1731 and lived to be 80 years old

*   Died 35 years to the day after signing the declaration

TLC10522 Copyright © Christine Boardman Moen

Student Example

*   Roger Sherman married Elizabeth Hartwell and had seven kids but

      Elizabeth died when she was only 34 years old

      Roger then married Rabecca Prescott with whom he had eight more

      kids for a total of 15 kids

*   He was most well known for being the only man to sign all 4 of the

      documents that established our nation

*   Born in 1721 and lived to be 72 years old

TLC10522 Copyright © Christine Boardman Moen

Todd

Graphic Organizer for Paragraph Developed with a List

Attention-Getter: quotations

Topic Sentence: Many different people signed the declaration of independence.

List Item 1:   Thomas McKean

   Detail: Most positions

List Item 2:   Caesar Rodney

   Detail: Riding ill

List Item 3:   George Read

   Detail: Signed D.I., signed U.S. Constitution twice

List Item 4:   Oliver Wolcott

   Detail: Bullet statue

List Item 5:   Samuel Huntington

   Detail: first president

List Item 6: (optional) William Williams	List Item 7: (optional) Roger Sherman
Detail: died 35 yr. to the day . . .	Detail: signed all 4 documents

Wrap-Up: These two states signers don't get recognized very often but they are . . .

Transitions and Signal Words:

Student Example

This is Todd's expanded version of the Paragraph Developed with Lists. This is Todd's first draft, and he chose to word process it so he could edit it easily at a later date.

"I shall always love my country." "A cause unspeakably important." "Pillar of the Revolution." These are quotes from and about men who signed our nation's most important document, The Declaration of Independence. Many different people signed the Declaration of Independence. Seven of these people were from the two states of Delaware and Connecticut. The three men from Delaware were Thomas McKean, Caesar Rodney and George Read. Thomas McKean was born in 1734 and lived to be 83 years old. During his lifetime he married Mary Borden with whom he had six children. After Mary died, He married Sarah Armitage and had five more children. He was most widely known for having held more major offices than any other American of his era. The second man to sign from Delaware was Caesar Rodney who was born in 1728 and lived to be 56 years old. He never married, but raised many of his relatives' children. His most well-known deed was when he rode a horse 80 miles in the night to Pennsylvania to vote for independence while he was extremely ill with cancer. The other person to sign from Delaware was a man by the name of George Read. He was born in 1733 and lived to be 65 years old, marrying Gertude Ross Till and they had no children. His largest accomplishment was not necessarily that he signed both the Declaration of Independence and the U.S. Constitution, but that he signed the U.S. Constitution twice, once for himself and once for Kickenson who was taken ill at the time. From Connecticut came four other signers. The first was Oliver Wolcott who was born in 1726 and lived to be 71 years old, marrying Laura Collins and having five children. He is well-known because when the head of a felled statue of King George III was sent to England, Wolcott took the rest of the statue home to Connecticut and had it melted down and made into bullets which were used against the British troops in battle. Another signer from Connecticut was Samuel Huntington. Born in 1731 and living to the age of 64 years old, he married Martha Devotion, had no children of his own, but raised some of his relatives' children. He is considered by some to be our nation's first president, largely because he was president of the First Continental Congress when our nation gained its freedom and became the Articles of the Confederation. The next man to sign from Connecticut was William Williams. He was born in the 1731 and lived to be 80 years old, marrying Mary Trumble and having three children. What he is most heavily remembered for is the fact that he died thirty five years to the day after signing the Declaration. The final signer of the Declaration of Independence from Connecticut was a man named Roger Sherman. He was born in 1721 and lived to 72 years old. During this time, he married Elizabeth Hartwell and had seven children, but Elizabeth died when she was 34 years old. He was the only man to ever sign all four documents by which our nation was established. These two states brought signers that were never made famous individually, but whose actions and influence have brought our country to where it is today.

TLC10522 Copyright © Christine Boardman Moen

Sift It	Lift It	Rachel
4	*ELEGY	
X	-elegy come from greek word elegia meaning "song of mourning," popular in greek tragedies	
	-elegiac stanza's = 4-line stanza (rhyme abab), elegy has no given pattern	
X	-first author of elegy is unknown	
X	-Mimnermus of Colophon (17 century) was thought to write the first elegy	
	-Over the centuries elegies went from writing of death to love to death (1611)	
	-famous elegists—Tibullus, Propertivs, Ovid, Clément Marot, Pierre de Ronsard & many others	
5	*PASTORAL POEM	
X	-comes from Latin word Pastor meaning "Shepherd"	
	-famous pastoral poets include the Ocritus, Virgil, Boccaccio, Christopher Marlowe & others	
	-poetry depicting life in the country	
	-different types—eclogues, idyl, amoebaean, pastourelle	
6	*SONNET	
X	-14 line poem, origin not completely known	
X	-theory around 1200 by Giacomo de Lentino	

Student Example

Sift It	Lift It		Rachel

_X_ -italian word sonetto "a little sound or song" that came from Latin

_____ sonus "a sound"

_1_ *FREE VERSE   vers libre French for free verse

_X_ -no rules to the poem   -Walt Whitman

_____ -appeared in the translation of the Bible

_X_ -gives the poet room to find his/her own writing rhythm

_3_ *SESTINA

_X_ -latin word sextus meaning "sixth"

_X_ -6 unrhymed stanzas, 6 lines each

_____ -concludes with a tercet (3 line stanza)

_2_ *Blank VERSE

_X_ -10 syllable lines, unrhymed (didn't end lines with rhyme)

_X_ -originated in late 16 century

_____ -usually has 5 accents in every line

_____ -Henry Howard is said to have been first poet in our language to use

_____ Blank verse

_1_ *HAIKU

_X_ -traditional Japanese poetry

_X_ -3 lines; 5 syllables, 7 syllables, 5 syllables

_____ -17 syllables all together

_____ -usually a nature, seasonal theme

_____ *PANTOUM

TLC10522 Copyright © Christine Boardman Moen

Graphic Organizer for
Paragraph Developed with a List

Attention-Getter: Writing poetry isn't something an average teenage boy does, but for Kevin Bolan it is the only thing that keeps him sain now that he has mono.

Topic Sentence: The author uses many different types of poems in "Shakespeare Bats Cleanup."

List Item 1: Haiku

    Detail: Traditional Japanese poem, 3 lines: 5 syllables, 7 syllables, 5 syllables

List Item 2: Blank verse

    Detail: 10 syllable lines, unrhymed, originated in 16th century

List Item 3: Sestina

    Detail: come from latin word sextus "6th." 6 unrhymed stanzas, 6 lines each

List Item 4: Elegy

    Detail: greek word elegia "song of mourning," first author unknown & mimnermus thought to write first elegy

List Item 5: Pastoral

    Detail: Latin word Pastor "Shepherd," depicts life in the country

List Item 6: Sonnet
(optional)

    Detail: 14 lines, Giacomode Lentino was said to write first sonnet, italian word sonetto "a little sound or song"

List Item 7: Free Verse
(optional)

    Detail: no rules, gives poet room to write his/her own way

Wrap Up: By reading "Shakespeare Bats Cleanup" the reader is influenced by many types of poems from many parts of the world

Transition:
Signal Words another, one example, also, last
Phrases

Student Example

This is Rachel's first draft, and she chose to word process it so she could edit it easily at a later date.

Shakespeare Bats Cleanup

Writing poetry isn't something an average teenager boy would do. But for Kevin Bolan it's the only thing that keeps him sane now that he has mono in Ron Koertge's book "Shakespeare Bats Cleanup." One example of these poems is a Haiku. A Haiku is a traditional Japanese poem with three lines: 5 syllables in the first line, 7 in the second line and 5 in the third line. Another type of poem used is Blank Verse poetry, which originated in the 16th century. A Blank Verse poem has 10 syllable lines and does not rhyme. Also a Sestina poem is written in the book. Sestina comes from the Latin word sextus meaning "sixth" and is written with 6 unrhymed stanzas, each one containing 6 lines. An Elegy poem comes from the Greek word meaning "Song of Mourning" and is written as an expression of the poet's sadness of death.   The first author of the elegy is unknown, but one theory is that Mimnermus of Colophon was the first poet of the elegy. A Pastoral Poem comes from the Latin word Pastor which means "shepherd." A pastoral poem pictures life in the country, usually on how peaceful it is. Sonnets come from the Italian word sonetto meaning "a little sound or song." The origin of the Sonnet is not completely known, but the theory is that in 1200 Giacomode Lentino invented it. The last type of poem used in "Shakespeare Bats Cleanup" is Free Verse. Free verse has no rules and gives the poet room to find his or her own rhythm to their poetry. By reading "Shakespeare Bats Cleanup" the reader is influenced by many types of poems from many parts of the world.

TLC10522 Copyright © Christine Boardman Moen

Student Example

Melissa

_____ There are 9 people from Pennsylvania to sign the declaration.

__X__ George Taylor—born in Ireland in 1716, came to america as an

_____ indentured servant, first had physical labor in an iron foundry,

_____ then once someone found he was educated he became clerk.

_____ Married Anne Savage; had 2 kids. An affair with housekeeper

_____ Naomi Smith, had 2 kids with her. 1764 elected to Pennsylvania

_____ legislature, signed it on August 2, 1776; left congress and

_____ retired of poor health, died Feb. 1781, 65 years old.

__X__ Benjamin Franklin—most well known, born in Boston

_____ Massachusetts in 1706, 15th in a family of 17. At the age of

_____ 10 had to work in family shop making candles and didn't like it.

_____ At 12 became an apprentice to older brother James, who was a

_____ printer. Ran away from home at 17 and settled in Philadelphia.

_____ Set up a printing business in 1729 and published his own news-

_____ paper, the Pennsylvania Gazette. Few years later Poor

_____ Richard's Almanac. Married Deborah Read in 1730, had Sally

_____ together and Franky who died of smallpox. Ben had 1 son by

_____ another woman, William. Invented Franklin stove, lightning rod,

_____ bifocals signed it at age 70.

_____

Student Example

Sift It   Lift It   Melissa

___X___ George Ross—uncle to Betsy Ross who made the flag, Born in Delaware in 1730, studied law

___X___ James Smith—born in Ireland he raised Pennsylvania's first volunteer company of revolutionary militia along with Samuel Adams and Ben Franklin was 1 of first people to call Continental Congress of American leaders

___X___ Robert Morris—financier of the Revolution created the bank of North America in Philadelphia, 1st successful bank.

___X___ James Wilson—1 of the 1st supreme court justices in 1789, appointed by George Washington

___X___ George Clymer—signed both the Declaration of Independence and Constitution, "dearest wish" was for his country to become independent. Only Roger Sherman of Connecticut, George Read of Delaware and him signed both

110

TLC10522 Copyright © Christine Boardman Moen